SAVING GOD

Saving God

Religion after Idolatry

MARK JOHNSTON

PRINCETON UNIVERSITY PRESS   PRINCETON & OXFORD

Published by Princeton University Press, 41 William Street,
    Princeton, New Jersey 08540
In the United Kingdom: Princeton University Press, 6 Oxford Street,
    Woodstock, Oxfordshire OX20 1TW

LIBRARY OF CONGRESS CATALOGING-IN-PUBLICATION DATA

Johnston, Mark, 1954–
    Saving God : religion after idolatry / Mark Johnston.
    p.   cm.
    Includes index.
    ISBN 978-0-691-14394-1 (hardcover : alk. paper)
    1. Religion—Philosophy. 2. Supernatural. 3. Natural theology.
4. Idolatry. I. Title.
    BL51.J75 2009
    210—dc22   2009012482

British Library Cataloging-in-Publication Data is available

This book has been composed in Minion

Printed on acid-free paper. ∞

press.princeton.edu

Printed in the United States of America

10 9 8 7 6 5 4 3 2 1

Frontispiece: *El Expolio—The Despoliation of Christ*, also known as *The Disrobing of Christ*, 1577–1579. Canvas, 129 × 160 cm. Cathedral, Toledo, Spain. Photo by Erich Lessing / Art Resource, NY Image Reference: ART213731

For my mum,

MARIE BRIGIT BRENNAN JOHNSTON

Contents

Preface

What follows is an essay, a sustained attempt to get something across, written more or less extempore. It uses the limited range of literary forms the author has at his disposal: quotation, argument, exegesis, midrash, mythic framing, the *via analogica*, readings against the grain, and the interrogation of the reader. (A poem would do so much better; there your man is Hopkins, and before him Rumi.)

The essay begins, dryly, with a simplified review of the semantics of names; and it gradually evolves into a sort of jeremiad. It contains some philosophy but is not a work of philosophy. My fellow philosophers will all too readily recognize the many places where I have declined the philosophically interesting pathways that branch off from what I say. Still less is it a work in academic theology, and I beg the forbearance of professional theologians as they read what must be, at so many points, glaringly at odds with their creedal commitments and their standard ways of explaining those commitments.

The work is offered simply as the expression of a certain sensibility. I give expression to it, at whatever risk, only because I hope that it has not entirely passed from the world. One kind of ideal reader would be an intelligent young person who is religious, but who feels that his or her genuine religious impulses are being strangled by what he or she is being asked to believe, on less than convincing authority, about the nature of reality. Such a person could begin with the postscript in order to see if what comes before might be in any way helpful, and so be worth the effort.

For those who are looking for a *philosophical* defense of the spiritual irrelevance of supernaturalism, one place to look is in my Hempel Lectures, entitled *Surviving Death*. Those lectures take up the crux of supernaturalist belief, namely, the belief in life after death.

SAVING GOD

Chapter 1

Is Your God Really God?

BELIEVING IN GOD

God is *God.*—KARL BARTH

Saving God is saving God *from us,* from our lazy and self-satisfied conviction that our conventional patterns of belief and worship could themselves capture God. God is transcendent; that is, God can come into view, if he comes into view at all, only as a result of his self-presentation. One consequence of this is the difficulty of knowing whether *even as a believer* you believe in God.

What is it to believe in God? Believing *in* God is not to be reduced to believing in the truth of the proposition that God exists. No doubt the Devil, if there were a Devil, would fully accept the proposition that his sworn enemy, God, exists; but nevertheless the Devil is a paradigm case of someone who does not believe *in* God. Believing in God is standing in a relation of faith and trust to the being who is God. Set aside for a moment the question of belief in the proposition that God exists. Consider instead this question:

"Do you believe in God?"

It is a question that many people, amazingly, are ready to answer affirmatively just by voicing or inspecting their own *inner* convictions.

I would like to begin by thanking Sarah-Jane Leslie for her encouragement and help throughout the project. Andrew Chignell, Jan Cover, James Edwards, and Jeff Stout provided invaluable comments and criticisms, and I hope that I have been able to improve the work as a result of all their efforts. Thanks also to Ian Malcolm, my editor at the Press, for working so hard to put the publication of this essay on an expedited schedule.

Yet relying on a purely subjective basis for answering, "Yes, I do believe in God" is odd, and perhaps disturbing. For it shows that the one who answers so quickly does not understand the question, and so does not understand just what it is to believe in God.

Suppose you look into your heart and see that there is *a god*, that is, an object of conventional prayer and worship, which you do believe in. How does that show that you believe in God? No amount of inspecting your own psychological state can itself determine whether you believe in God, as opposed to *a god*.

Indeed, we shall soon discover that you could believe that there is a God, and believe that your god is God, and believe in your god, but still fail miserably in believing in God. The first three conditions you can determine by looking into your heart; the fourth is, in a certain way, beyond your immediate ken. It requires a certain success in hitting the correct target. Or, more exactly, it requires the arrow of God to have had you, or your religious tradition, as its target.

There is, then, a question as to whether your god is really God. This is an objective question that transcends what is settled by your own psychological state, your introspectible state of belief in and devotion toward any particular god made salient to you by this or that religious tradition.

Here is an induction from past cases which must worry anyone who supposes that he can just announce that he believes in *God*. There is a confused syncretism that identifies Yahweh with the Holy Trinity (or one member of it) and also with Allah, despite the overwhelming scriptural evidence to the contrary. If we set that confusion aside, then, for the reasons articulated at various points in what lies below, whatever one's monotheistic persuasion might be, one must recognize that many subjectively sincere "believers" who announce that they believe in God, do not in fact believe in God. For, as the unconfused Christian would say, it is the Holy Trinity, the Triune God, at once Father, Son and Holy Spirit, who is God, and these people believe in Yahweh or Allah. Or, as the unconfused Jew would say (if he could but speak the name "Yahweh"), it is Yahweh alone who is God, and these people believe in Allah or the Holy Trinity. Or, as the unconfused Muslim would say, it is Allah alone who is God, and these people do not believe in Allah, but in Yahweh or the Holy Trinity.

We may summarize these charges and countercharges like this: "These people may be utterly sincere, but their god is not God. When they announce that they believe in God, they are indeed sincere, but they are mistaken. You cannot tell whether you believe in God, as opposed to a god, just by looking into your heart."

The charge echoes back on those who make it: "How do you know that *your* god is God? Clearly, no amount of inspecting *your* own subjective psychological state, and giving voice to *your* belief in and devotion toward any particular object of conventional worship and prayer will settle that question."

This simple point is obscured by a widespread syncretistic theology that automatically identifies the gods of the major theisms. I shall argue that the reasons against this identification are manifest and clear, even a cursory glance at the scriptures of Judaism, Christianity, and Islam shows that the children of Abraham have come to address themselves to different gods. And it is a point of logic that *at most* one of these could be God.

Nevertheless, a syncretistic confusion dominates modern theology because of a kind of wishful thinking, a form of thinking in which a technical theological claim (the numerical identity of the gods of the monotheisms) is the illegitimate offspring of decent and widely held desires. All decent people want to avoid sectarian violence; all decent people want to respect others, and that means respecting their deeply held beliefs, and all decent believers want to cooperate with people of other faiths in the midst of the great challenges that face us all. These are very important ends. Still, our intense desires for these worthy ends do not in any way justify the belief that "we all worship the same God."

What could or would justify that belief is a cold, hard look at what we *do* worship. One reason why that is a difficult thing to do, one reason why reflex syncretism is so comforting, is that taking a cold, hard look at what we do worship would leave *us* with the anxious questions: Do *we* really believe in *God*? Is *our* god really God?

As we shall see, the major monotheisms originally defined themselves in part by denigrating the gods of others. The charge of idolatry, of worshipping a false god, is part of the self-defining rhetoric of monotheism. It is the charge one makes against others because they do not worship one's own god, who (one supposes) is *God*. Monotheism without the charge of idolatry is a bit like *Othello* without Desdemona. There would be little there to move the plot along.

To begin to understand the question "Do you believe in God?" we need to understand this charge of idolatry, and its role in the self-defining rhetoric of the major monotheisms.

First, however, it may be helpful to dwell a little on the meaning of "God."

ON THE "NAMES" OF GOD

If we are to understand the question "Do you believe in God?" and so understand what it would be to believe in God, the first thing to understand is that "God," if it is a name at all, is not an ordinary proper name like "Judas Maccabeus," "Samuel Johnson," or "Kurt Gödel."

As the philosopher Saul Kripke established, we can use ordinary proper names perfectly competently even when we have quite false ideas about the bearers of those names. It is not part of being a competent user of an ordinary proper name that we associate some true description with the name, a description that the bearer happens to satisfy, and satisfy uniquely. To take Kripke's example, all I may take myself to know of Kurt Gödel is that he proved the incompleteness of arithmetic; but if in truth he plagiarized this proof from a certain Fritz Schmidt, who was the one who actually proved the incompleteness of arithmetic, then I still have, and this needs some appreciation, *a false belief about Kurt Gödel, not a true belief about Fritz Schmidt.* The descriptive content I associate with the name "Kurt Gödel" does not make that name pick out Schmidt in the imagined situation, even though in the imagined situation that descriptive content is true of Schmidt and not of Gödel.[1]

Just as I get to refer to Gödel by "Gödel" even in a state of ignorance or confusion about who exactly Gödel is, I also get to refer to a particular man by "Judas Maccabeus" because that name is a transformation of an original Jewish name that was used to dub a particular human being at a particular time, and was passed down through a certain lin-

---

1. See Saul A. Kripke, *Naming and Necessity* (Harvard University Press, 1980).

eage of use, a lineage of use where the common intention is to employ the name "Judas Maccabeus," or its original Hebrew form, to refer to the man who was originally so dubbed. I can connect to that lineage of use of the original name by way of using the English transformation of the name. I thereby refer to the man Judas Maccabeus, even though I might have thoroughly false beliefs about him.

Imagine, for example, that I confusedly think he is the same man as Judas Iscariot. Even so, the content of my confusion would be that Judas Maccabeus is Judas Iscariot. I could not be confused in that way unless I was still referring to Judas Maccabeus by "Judas Maccabeus" *despite my confusion about the facts.*

Considerations akin to these have been widely taken to establish at least this: in order to be competent with ordinary names, you need not be the master of some specific descriptive material that the bearer of the name uniquely satisfies. What you need to do is intentionally connect to a chain of reference that leads back to an original use of the name in question, a use in which the name was given to its bearer.

Could it be like that with "God"? Could you refer to and think about God, the true God, even if the descriptive content of your associated beliefs were not true of any being in particular, or true of something other than God? The syncretistic theology mentioned earlier seems to assume just that, and in doing so, this standard syncretism appears to treat "God" as on a par with an ordinary proper name like "Kurt Gödel" or "Samuel Johnson." If "God" were an ordinary proper name, then the various monotheisms might succeed in referring to, addressing, and worshipping the same God, *despite* their very different and inconsistent collective beliefs about his nature and intentions. For ordinary proper names are forgiving in just this way, as Kripke showed. Gödel's mother and a logic student who hears about him for the first time will have thought about Gödel in utterly different, and perhaps even disjoint and inconsistent ways. Still, it is Gödel they are thinking of.

On this model, all the adherents of the different monotheisms would need to do is intend to connect with a chain of reference that leads back to some primordial dubbing of some being with some original, say Hebrew, form of the name "God." Then they could think about the being who is God in very different, and even confused and false, ways.

However, that is not how "God" works. In the scriptures, no one actually turns up and says anything like "I am to be called by *the name* 'God.'" No one says anything like "I hereby introduce *the name* 'God' as the name of THIS very impressive being." There is no original dubbing of someone or something as "God," a dubbing that we now can hope to fall back on. When the English translations of the scriptures refer to a being as "God" (the title associated with the Hebrew terms *el, elohim, elohay*), the point of the texts they translate is not to use "God" as the *proper name* of some very impressive being, but to convey something about the elevated status of that being.

To be sure, there is one dramatic act of divine self-naming in the Hebrew scriptures, but the name in question is not "God" or any name of which that is the translation. Exodus tells us that a divine being presented himself to Moses and dubbed himself "Yahweh," a nature-revealing designator often translated as "I am" or "I am who am":

> "But," said Moses to God, "when I go to the Israelites and say to them, 'The god of your fathers has sent me to you,' if they ask me, 'What is his name?' what am I to tell them?" God replied, "I am who am." Then he added, "This is what you shall tell the Israelites: I AM sent me to you . . . This is My eternal name, and this is how I am to be recalled for all generations." (Exodus 3:14–15)

Even if, as the passage asserts, Yahweh is in fact God, the name "Yahweh" does not mean the same as "God." For it is coherent to doubt, as the second-century theologian Marcion did, whether Yahweh is in fact God. Marcion also doubted that the god who appeared to Abraham was God. If Marcion was wrong about this, then his mistakes were not about the meanings of words. They would be mistakes as to the theological facts of the matter. This itself entails that "Yahweh" does not mean "God," and that "God" does not mean "the god who appeared to Abraham." If those were equivalences in meaning, then there would be no room for the relevant factual mistakes.

In fact, it is quite unclear whether "God," as we now use it, is a *name* at all, as opposed to a compressed title, in effect something like "the

Supreme Being" or "the Most High." Notice that the so-called Names of God that appear in the Hebrew scriptures are more like titles or honorific descriptions intended to highlight aspects of the nature of the god of Israel. The first such godly "name" appears in Genesis 1:1—

In the beginning *elohim* created the heaven and the earth.

—and *elohim* is just the plural form of a Hebrew root with a meaning that is something like "divine might" or "supremacy." Throughout the Hebrew scriptures *elohim*, along with its cognate *elohay* and its simpler form *el*, is used to mean "god" or "the god of" as in the following:

elohim kedoshim, the holy god
elohay elohim, the god of all gods
elohay kedem, the god of the beginning
elohay yishi, the god who provides salvation
el elyon, the most high
el echad, the one god
el shaddai, the almighty god

These are clearly intended as either titles or honorific descriptions, whose point is in part to distinguish *el yisrael*, the god of Israel, from other, lesser gods.[2]

If "God" as we now use it is a name in any sense, it clearly does not function like an ordinary proper name. In its function, it is closest to what philosophers call a *descriptive name*, a name that in some way

---

2. One might describe "*el*" as a functional expression, comparable in the way it works to the English expression "the friend of," which is an expression that connects with names, and phrases to generate various descriptions, as in "the friend of Samuel Johnson," "The friend of the downtrodden," and "the friend of the court." Notice that there is no meaningful way to abstract out "Friend" from these descriptions, and use it as a name of one or another of the persons in question.

This raises a scholarly question that goes beyond the bounds of the present discussion: Given that there is no capitalization in Hebrew, how far does the continual reappearance of the capitalized forms "Theos," "Deus," "Gott," "God," and the like, throughout the translations of the earliest Hebrew scriptures, represent something of a mistranslation, due to the reading back of a later monotheistic idea, essentially *our* idea, of God? Would it not be better to amend many of the occurrences of "God" in the standard translations to read instead as "the god" and "the god of . . ."?

abbreviates a description and so is tied to that description for its meaning. Perhaps this was true of the name "Hesperus" (or rather the name for which it is a transliteration) as it was originally introduced. "Hesperus" was introduced more or less as an abbreviation for a description like "the actual thing that appears in the night sky as the brightest heavenly body, after the moon." For a while after the introduction of that name in that way, you couldn't have been competent with that name without being disposed to treat that description, or something like it, as the criterion for determining the reference of the name. Then we may suppose that the connection to the original description faded away so that only those who call to mind the Latin and Greek roots of the name would explicitly associate the description with the name. The name "Hesperus" ceased to be a descriptive name and became more like an ordinary proper name.

Here is a fact about *descriptive* names: you can't use such a name with its ordinary meaning without being disposed to use the description associated with the name to determine the reference of the name. And here is an even more relevant fact: you don't get to refer to something by a descriptive name unless the thing in question actually satisfies the associated description. During the period when "Hesperus" was a descriptive name, if in truth it *had been* that Mars was brighter in the night sky than Venus, then "Hesperus" would have denoted Mars, not Venus. You don't get "forgiven" for making crucial factual errors in the case of descriptive names, for the reference of such names is just that of their semantically associated descriptions.

So suppose that "God" is a descriptive name whose associated description is something like "the Highest One" and suppose, just for the sake of illustration, that in fact it is Allah and not the Holy Trinity who is the Highest One. Then it will follow that in their characteristic acts of worship, Christians are not worshipping God, because they do not worship Allah. *Christians would not just have false beliefs about God.* In the prayers and liturgical practices that are distinctive of the Christian religion, directed as they are essentially to the Father, the Son, and the Holy Spirit, *Christians would not even be addressing God.* And when Christians call on God *as such*, they would, unbeknownst to themselves, be calling not on the Holy Trinity, but on Allah. And as the Holy Koran says, they would thereby be offering him a mighty insult in supposing he is a trinity of persons.

Thus if "God" is either an abbreviated title or a descriptive name, then the meaning of "God" is very unforgiving, unforgiving in a way that can only intensify the anxieties associated with the question

"Do you believe in *God*?"

We might develop those anxieties in this way. Once you understand the meaning of "God," you should be able to see that even if you believe that God (the Highest One) exists, and even if that belief is true, and even though you sincerely believe in a god, *you may be very far from believing in God.* The wrong god may have captured your attention and your heart. Believing in God is *not a mere psychological state.* It is more akin to an achievement. For it involves hitting the mark, that is, directing your faith and trust toward the one who is in fact the Highest One.

This means that you are in no better position just to decide to believe in God than you are in a position just to decide to win your first marathon without ever having trained for it. And our position may be worse than that, for winning a marathon is an individual achievement, something that lies within the capacity of a few of us. But there is no chance of believing in God, unless God has disclosed himself to us. The achievement of believing in God can come about only in the wake of God's self-revelation. And no religion, no practice or set of beliefs, however appealing, can make itself enlivened by God's self-revelation. The Highest One cannot be manipulated by any cult; his appearance is a grace of fortune. To think otherwise is idolatrous, as we shall see.

Suppose that someone dedicates a temple to "the Highest One, Whoever or Whatever That Is." (Someone, somewhere, should do this noble thing.) Presumably he believes that there is a Highest One, and builds the temple as an invitation to the Highest One to make itself manifest. Still, this noble person need not have any belief *in* the Highest One, that is, God. For merely building the temple as an invitation would not yet constitute a relation of faith and trust in God. To have that, not only do you have to understand the meaning of "God" and believe that there is a God, you would also have to focus on the right god—as it were, the right object of conventional worship—as "God." *And it re-*

mains a live possibility that no object of conventional worship is, as yet, God.

That is why belief in God may be a much rarer thing than has been almost universally supposed.

And it leaves the question: What could possibly count as evidence that you believe in *God?* It can seem surprising that this question can be asked. But it is even more surprising that the answers are not ready to hand.

The best thing a believer can say in response to the question "Do you believe in God?" is "I can only hope that I do. I can only hope that I actually stand in a tradition in which God has genuinely revealed himself."

Think of this essay as an exploration of how things look when that hope seeks understanding.

THE MEANING OF "GOD" AND THE COMMON CONCEPTION OF GOD

The history of monotheism was for a long period of time the history of Jewish monotheism, and we would do well to look to the descriptions that are applied to Yahweh in the Hebrew scriptures, by way of asserting that Yahweh is indeed, as we would now put it, God.

Descriptions like "*el yisrael,*" or "the god of Israel," are not of the relevant sort, for it remains a substantial question, a question to be settled by the truth or falsity of the Jewish faith, and not by the meaning of words, whether *el yisrael* is God.

What we therefore need, in order to clarify the meaning of "God" thought of as a descriptive name, is a conjunction of descriptions, call it *D*, such that it no longer seems a substantial question whether D is God. Here are the sorts of descriptions that bid fair to be included in D:

> *elohay elohim,* the god over all gods
> *elohay yishi,* the god who provides salvation
> *el elyon,* the Most High

The god of gods, the Most High who gives salvation now it no longer seems a substantial question whether that being would, if it existed, be God.

The substantial question then becomes: Who or what is God?

Here we are close to the meaning of "God" as we now use that term. But we can simplify and refine this account. Notice that the honorific description *elohay elohim*, the god over all the gods, is an expression not so much of Jewish monotheism, the belief in one god, but of what scholars call Jewish "henotheism": the belief that there is a god preeminent among the gods. This is indeed how Yahweh seems to be depicted in Psalm 82 and at Deuteronomy 32:8–9 and elsewhere.

In Psalm 82, Yahweh is described as calling together the heavenly council of the lesser gods (*elohim*) that he has placed over the gentiles.

He presides in the divine council; in the midst of the gods he holds judgment

Henotheism is a stage on the journey from polytheism to monotheism, a journey that is completed with the cry "There is no god but God," or, as the psalmist puts it,

All the gods of the gentiles are idols. (Psalm 96:5)

Standing at the end of this journey, we no longer conceive of God as the head of a council of gods. We do not think of God as the god of gods, or if we do think of him, say, as presiding over angelic hierarchies, at least we think of this as only the outer manifestation of his true superiority as the Highest One in the sense of the Most Perfect Being.

Is that description on its own adequate to capture the sense of "God"? It is conceivable that mathematical reality taken as a whole is the Most Perfect Being, because it is utterly complete, beautiful, self-contained, and inherently intelligible, in a way that cannot be approximated by anything in the spatiotemporal realm. Even if this were true, there would be something unserious about using "God" as a name for mathematical reality. This is *because the existence and nature of mathe-*

matical reality in no way bears on our salvation.[3] The same could be said to those who believe that there is such a thing as the Universe considered as an ordered whole, the Cosmos if you will, and who hold that the Cosmos is in some relevant sense the Most Perfect Being. It would be forced, even perhaps idle, to call the Cosmos "God" unless its nature in some way leaves a special place for our salvation.

So, for example, when Baruch Spinoza in the *Ethics* calls the one substance that is the Cosmos "Deus sive Natura," that is, "God or Nature," this is not idle because Spinoza finds within the Cosmos a definite path to salvation, a condition that he calls the intellectual love of God, a condition in which one experiences freedom from the bondage of destructive emotions and inadequate ideas. Otherwise, Spinoza's appropriation of the term "God" would be a forced addition to his philosophical monism, the thesis that everything is a manifestation of the one substance.

This is not because salvation enters into the meaning of the descriptive name "God." The name or title "God" does not literally mean

the Highest One, and the one from whom flows our salvation.

For it is thinkable, indeed more than thinkable, that God exists but has no interest in our salvation.

Still, the three monotheisms—Judaism, Christianity, and Islam—are essentially religions of *salvation history,* religions whose revelations purportedly show God in search of humanity, in order to save that peculiar creature. Monotheism is in part the extraordinary idea that *we* matter that much to the Highest One. The very idea of salvation history is thus extraordinary; in fact it is utterly shocking, and so it is clearly not guaranteed by the idea of God as such. That God is our salvation is monotheism's shocking and very substantial claim, which is to say that it does not follow from the meaning of "God," the title or descriptive name whose *meaning* is best understood as given by a description like "the Highest One."[4]

---

3. The Pythagoreans might have disagreed. But then, the little we know of Pythagoreanism makes it look more like a quasi-religion than like a mere philosophy.

4. Semanticists will ask: Do I mean "the actual Highest One," so that "God" would denote the same being in any possible situation, even one in which a Higher One than any actual one exists?

Even so, anyone using the title or descriptive name "God" in an attempt to connect with the monotheistic tradition should bear in mind that it would be unserious to assert that God exists without supposing that there is a Highest One from whom our salvation flows. For that is the *common conception* of God in the major monotheisms.

If only we could say what salvation is, we could then explain this common conception, in order to further explore the question of who or what God is.

One advantage of this approach is that we would then not have to prematurely settle questions of existence. Instead, we could treat the major monotheisms "phenomenologically"—which is to say, we could bracket the questions of whether Allah exists or whether Yahweh exists or whether the Holy Trinity exists. We could take the religious sensibilities and orientations associated with the worship of each of these beings *on their own terms*, and then ask: Which of these beings, *if it existed*, would be God, that is, the Highest One, from whom or from which flows our salvation?

What Is Salvation?

That may seem to be a pointless approach, unless we can find a relatively neutral account of salvation, an account that does not stack the deck in favor of one or the other of the major monotheisms. But how could there be a neutral account of salvation, neutral across the major monotheisms? After all, Judaism has for most of its history shown little interest in the afterlife, Islam allows itself vivid descriptions of material and sensual reward in the afterlife, and Christianity offers us the Beatific Vision, understood as partial participation in the inner life of the Holy Trinity. These accounts of salvation clearly conflict in their concrete details. Any neutral account of salvation would have to be a higher-order account, which the three monotheisms could be seen as filling out, each in its own particular way.

I do mean "the actual Highest One," but I also take it that if this description picks out anything, it picks out an entity that is such that there *could not* be a Higher in this world or in any other. There is a certain very High minimum that would have to be met by something if it is to be "the Highest One." I take it that this is part of the understanding of "the Most High" and the like. But I am setting that aside here in the interests of brevity.

The neutral account, if it is to illuminate the common conception of God, understood as

the Highest One, from whom (or from which) flows our salvation

should satisfy another condition. It should be a characterization that is at least *comprehensible* to unbelievers. For at least some unbelievers understand the common conception and use it to express their unbelief.

We might admit a third constraint. It is not just the monotheistic religions that offer salvation; the same is arguably true of Buddhism and Hinduism, though of course the concrete conception of salvation in these religions is very different from what we find in the monotheisms. In fact, Buddhism vividly disjoins salvation from any idea of the Highest One; salvation lies in the overcoming of anxious desire by means of the Eightfold Path. This is the essential antitheism of Buddhism; it breaks apart the common conception of the three monotheisms, by disconnecting salvation from the Highest One. If that is the right characterization of how Buddhism stands to the three monotheisms, then there ought to be a neutral account of salvation that makes some sense of what is going on in Buddhism as well.

Salvation versus Spiritual Materialism

In offering a first pass at a neutral account of salvation, we might begin with the idea of spiritual materialism. "Spiritual materialism" is a term from the sixties, used then to denote the consumerist attitude of self-described "seekers" who were always on the lookout for the latest, most fashionable guru or meditation technique or method of self-transformation.

The implied criticism was that the spiritually "materialistic" seekers had undergone no fundamental change in their orientation to life but had simply taken up the hobby of self-improvement, with its endless opportunities for self-worship. The ordinary unredeemed self remained at the center of things; the same lust for advantage and desire for power that drive people in ordinary life were simply projected onto the supposedly spiritual realm disclosed by LSD or Zen or Vedanta or Buddhism or Transcendental Meditation.

It was a charge of religious fraudulence in some ways akin to the old charge of idolatry made by the monotheisms as they defined themselves against their own polytheistic and henotheistic origins.

What makes one religious orientation fraudulent and another authentic? In the context of monotheism the primary conception of religious fraudulence has centered on idolatry, that is, worshipping the wrong god, or the right god in the wrong way. But the more popular religious orientations of the sixties were varieties of Buddhism along with practical meditation techniques drawn from Hinduism. These were not essentially theistic orientations, so the charge of religious fraudulence inherent in the term "spiritual materialism" was not the charge of idolatry. What was it, and what was the related conception of religious authenticity, which could extend even to nontheistic religious practice?

Genuine or true religion must be genuinely directed upon what religion is for. There are certain large-scale structural defects in human life that no amount of psychological adjustment or practical success can free us from. These include arbitrary suffering, aging (once it has reached the corrosive stage), our profound ignorance of our condition, the isolation of ordinary self-involvement, the vulnerability of everything we cherish to time and chance, and, finally, to untimely death. (Yes, death can be a release, but only when suffering or corrosive aging has already undermined the goods that an untimely death would have otherwise destroyed.)

The religious or redeemed life is a form of life in which we are reconciled to these large-scale defects of ordinary life. I do not say that redemption or salvation in this sense must require that all the wounds are healed, or that everything has turned out, or will turn out, for the best. There are things so horrible and tragic that nothing that subsequently happens can diminish the tragedy or the horror; and anyone who tells you otherwise is just making it up, or relying on someone else who just made it up. Worse, the attempt to put an otherworldly frame around such things so they seem not to be the tragedies or the horrors that they manifestly are, borders on the childish and the obscene. Still, the idea of salvation says that even in the face of such things there must be a way to go on, keeping faith in the importance of goodness, and an openness to love.

Now there are certain virtues (i.e., beneficial dispositions of character) that religious practice deepens. The virtues in question somehow reconcile us to the large-scale defects of human life. Herein lies the distinction between the "ordinary" and the so-called theological virtues. Ordinary virtue—self-confidence, flexibility, openness, self-directed irony, perseverance, fair-dealing, moderation, and good judgment—takes life on its own unredeemed terms and makes the most of it by way of these dispositions of character often so beneficial in ordinary life. By contrast, the so-called theological virtues change the terms of life. Thus, in the Christian tradition, faith, hope, and love are cited not merely as intensifications of ordinary virtue, but as the conditions of a transformed or redeemed life.

That might help us understand the charge of spiritual materialism, even as it applies outside the theistic religions. The spiritual materialist is inauthentic in his engagement with religion, and with his spiritual quest or search, precisely because he simply turns his ordinary unredeemed desires toward some supposedly spiritual realm. However intense his experiences, they do not deepen in him the theological virtues that constitute the change of orientation that makes for a new life.

Salvation, understood as the goal of religious or spiritual life, is a new orientation that authentically addresses the large-scale defects of human life, and thereby provides a reservoir of energy otherwise dissipated in denial of, and resistance to, necessary suffering. Salvation, so understood, is not the mere feeling or conviction that you are "saved." It is a new form of life.

If there is a God that corresponds to the outlook of the three monotheisms, then it must be that, somehow, in properly relating to the Highest One, a person acquires such a new orientation and is *eo ipso* saved. Belief in God is not a matter of believing in the proposition that he exists; it is an orientation in which the Highest One comes into view, with salvific effect.

Real atheism, as opposed to mere disbelief in Yahweh, Allah, and the Holy Trinity, is the conviction either that there is no Highest One, or that if there were there is no reason to suppose that it could, or would, offer us salvation. That leaves one religious option, even for a real atheist, namely, finding an orientation out of which one can live, without denying or resisting the necessary suffering that is inherent in the large-scale defects of human life.

Then there are those whom we might call, in the fashion of Richard Rorty's own self-description, the "religiously tone-deaf": those who simply find these remarks about necessary suffering and the large-scale structural defects of human life to be odd or overblown or, perhaps, just in bad taste. I wish them well, but I feel obliged to warn them not to waste their time by reading on.

Chapter 2

The Idolatrous Religions

THE BAN ON IDOLATRY

> "But," said Moses to God, "when I go to the Israelites and
> say to them, 'The god of your fathers has sent me to you,'
> if they ask me, 'What is his name?' what am I to tell
> them?" God replied, "I am who am." Then he added,
> "This is what you shall tell the Israelites: I AM sent me to
> you."—EXODUS 3:13–14

> I am the Lord your God, who brought you out of Egypt,
> out of the land of slavery. You shall have no other gods
> before me. You shall not make for yourself a graven image,
> or any likeness of anything that is in heaven above, or that
> is in the earth beneath, or that is in the water under the
> earth; you shall not bow down to them or serve them; for
> I, the Lord your God, am a jealous God, visiting the
> iniquity of the fathers upon the children to the third and
> the fourth generation of those who hate me, but showing
> steadfast love to thousands of those who love me and keep
> my commandments.—EXODUS 20:3–6

How can the very one who introduces himself as "I AM," in Exodus 3,
be the proprietary and jealous god of Exodus 20, who so fears Israel's
cuckolding him with the gods of the pagans that he threatens to visit
"the iniquity of the fathers upon the children to the third and the fourth
generation"? Is it that the anthropocentric accretions of Exodus 20 have
already obscured the real nature of the Highest One, so that the original
ban on idolatry is itself refracted through an idolatrous prism?

That, however, unnaturally limits our questioning to Judaism; for
directly related questions also arise about Christianity and Islam. The
crucial thing in all this is not to insult anyone's genuine faith, but to

display at each point the historical sediments of our collective resistance to True Divinity. The sacred scriptures often exhibit a self-incriminating character, in that they serve also to expose the idolatrous potential of even the ostensible true believers. And this is no special virtue of the Hebrew scriptures.

So, to take the Christian case, Paul, in his panegyric to love at 1 Corinthians 13, in effect represents the central elements of first-century Christian religion, namely, speaking in tongues, prophesying, having a faith that moves mountains, understanding the mysteries, giving away one's possessions to the poor, and even martyrdom, as in themselves "nothing."

> If I speak in the tongues of men and of angels, but have not love, I am only a resounding gong or a clanging cymbal. If I have the gift of prophecy and can fathom all mysteries and all knowledge, and if I have a faith that can move mountains, but have not love, I am nothing. If I give all I possess to the poor and surrender my body to the flames, but have not love, I gain nothing.

Nothing? The immanent and heroic form of first-century Christian life is nothing? Yes, nothing, zero, a waste, if it is not animated by *agape*. Are we not here reminded of the guiding rule for serious thought about religion, the rule so well articulated by Karl Barth, when he wrote that religion is faithlessness; or, as we might put it, that religion's natural character, even at its humanly heroic best, is to be a form of substitution of the inessential for the essential, the god for God? As Barth puts it, "true religion" is like "redeemed sinner"; even after redemption the sinner remains a sinner, and even if a religion is true, it will be naturally filled with the inessential and the false. If there is any religion that is true, then this is because of something wholly extraneous to it, namely, God's activity in animating the religion.[1]

---

1. See sec. 17 of Karl Barth's *Church Dogmatics*: "The Revelation of God as the Abolition of Religion." An extremely helpful retranslation and introduction to this work is provided by Garrett Green under the title *On Religion* (T & T Clarke, 2006). See especially pt. 2 of sec. 17, "Religion as Faithlessness" (53–84 in Green), and the long footnote to pt. 3, "The True Religion," where Barth makes the point about 1 Corinthians 13.

From any ordinary, which is to say unredeemed, point of view, True Divinity *ought* to be resisted, and its intimations domesticated. Were the experience of True Divinity to break through, something unprecedented would be asked of us in the name of a higher authenticity; and we would stand accused of already evading this higher demand in the living of our self-involved lives.

Where it is not simple worship of lifeless idols, idolatry is an attempt to domesticate the experience of Divinity, to put it to some advantage in a still unredeemed life. And then the true God slips away.

To the extent that the actually existing religions embody one or another version of this kind of compromise, they are idolatrous. To comprehend one's own religion is not just to comprehend its dogmas and rituals. It involves bringing into clear view the religion's characteristic way of resisting the Divine: its way of redeploying its supposed foundational experiences of Divinity in the service of a reinvented worldliness on which one's religious community has itself come to depend.

IDOLATRY AS PERVERSE WORSHIP

As Yahweh's first commandment suggests, one can fall into idolatry without worshipping graven images. The sun and the moon are not graven images; even so, sun worshippers and moon worshippers are paradigmatic idolaters. The Hebrew for idolatry, *avodah zarah,* means strange, perverse, or alien worship. Worship can be perverse even if it is directed, not to man-made images, but to a lesser god, a god who is not the Highest One.

So although the Decalogue immediately goes on to repudiate graven images, Yahweh's prior and first commandment delivered to Moses on Mount Sinai insists that the Israelites shall have no other *gods* before him. Yahweh presents himself as the Most High; that is why it is idolatrous to worship other gods in his place. It would be idolatrous even if

---

Barth believes that there could be a false religion wholly isomorphic in practice and belief to the true religion. See his remarkable comparison between Pure Land Buddhism and Protestantism in pt. 3 of *On Religion.* This is the anticipation of the lessons of "twin-earth" in the theology of the thirties; when it comes to religion, Barth is the original "externalist" in the philosopher's sense.

the gods in question were genuine but lesser divinities, powerful inter-mediate spiritual beings, like the sun *god* or the moon *god*.

In giving this first commandment, Yahweh knew his audience well. There is considerable evidence that the Israelites who followed Moses into the desert continued to view the old gods of Egypt and its adjacent territories not as fictions, but as genuine spiritual beings. The Israelites were still inclined to propitiate these old gods. The emerg-ing monotheism of the Israelites *was* more akin to "henotheism," the belief in a supreme deity as well as various lesser divinities; and so Yahweh announces that he is a jealous God, not to be betrayed by Isra-el's wandering eye. Yahweh's later prophets Hosea, Jeremiah, and Eze-kiel will go on to repeatedly warn Israel that she faces a terrible cost for what amounts to adulterous whoring with the lesser and alien gods of the other tribes.[2]

Through these prophets, Yahweh primarily insists not on monothe-ism, the belief that there is but one god, but rather on "monolatry," exclusive worship of himself because he is the Highest One. To worship lesser spiritual beings would not only be an insult to the Highest One, the blasphemous element in idolatry; it would also be a wasteful misdi-rection of spiritual energies. The idolatrous cannot have access to true salvation, which consists in the right relation to the Highest One.

Graven Images and the Highest One

Why not simply take the ban on idolatry to be given by the second, more obvious, commandment, which merely proscribes graven images? Why yoke the second commandment together with the first, and thereby treat the proscription against graven images as only a part of the total expression of the ban on idolatry? What is the real connection between the two commandments that are traditionally taken to forbid idolatrous worship?

---

2. On the explicitly sexual character of Yahweh's jealousy, see, for example, the book of Hosea, especially the denunciation of Israel as the "wife of whoredom," and modern commentaries on this theme, such as Gerlinde Baumann's *Love and Violence* (Liturgical Press, 2003), which dwells on the awkward question of how Yahweh can allow his prophet to call for Israel to be, in effect,

The first commandment, the demand that no god be placed before Yahweh, serves to explain the second, and not just because the resort to graven images was the most likely way in which the Israelites would engage with the old gods.

What, after all, is so bad about a graven image? If it is permissible to speak of the right hand of God, why can't one model it in wood or bronze?[3]

Hollywood voodoo and other forms of cartoon fetishism aside, it is rare to find someone who actually *worships* a graven image as such. The idol worshipper need not, and typically will not, identify the graven image with his god. He is likely to know that even though there is, say, only one Horus, the Egyptian falcon god of the sky, there are many sacred statues of Horus. Still, he is an idolater if he worships a statue of Horus as an embodiment of the god.

The Horus worshipper's idolatry cannot consist simply in the fact that he reveres a given statue of Horus, in the way, say, that an irreligious admirer of Michelangelo might nevertheless revere the *Pietà*. Nor can it consist in the fact that the statue puts him in mind of Horus, to whom he might then pray, say in the way that the *Pietà* might cause a Christian to pray to Christ, or in the way that the sight of the Ark of the Covenant in the Temple might have been the cause of worship directed to Yahweh.

Worship, at least in the sense in which idolatry is perverse worship, is not mere reverence for the idol, and is not merely the ritualistic exploitation of the idol understood as an image or representation of the god, his characteristics, or his acts.

To worship something in the relevant sense, that is, the sense in which idolatry is *perverse* worship, is in crucial part to declare fealty or devotion to its will. This is done in a speech act or ritual act, an act that the object of worship is supposedly able to appreciate. (Prostration is thus

---

gang-raped, as in Ezekiel 16. In Jeremiah 13:26, Yahweh himself threatens sexual violence against Israel: "I will lift up your skirts over your face, and your shame will be seen."

3. Compare Avishai Margalit and Moshe Halbertal's very fine work *Idolatry* (Harvard University Press, 1992), which puts the same question about depictions of God. Wittgenstein may have suggested the answer when he asked: How is it that we can speak of the hand of God, but not his fingernail?

the exemplary sign of worship, for it is the bodily expression of complete fealty.) To commit idolatry, then, the idol worshipper must see the idol as not just a signifier or representation of the god, but as an *embodiment* of the god. The god is HERE, somehow contained where the idol is, and so can appreciate the proffered act of fealty made before the idol.

There is the rub. For graven images or idols are human creations, and if they were embodiments of the god, then human craftsmen would have influence over when and where the god is embodied. So the god embodied in the idol cannot be the Highest One, for no human being, and certainly no crafter of images, could have influence over when and where the Highest One is embodied. With this connective tissue in place, the second commandment can be understood as a corollary of the first. To worship graven images is *eo ipso* to turn one's attention away from the Highest One toward supposed deities whose embodiment is under the influence or control of human beings. To make graven images for such worship is either to suppose that one could manipulate the Highest One, or, at the very least, to collaborate with one's customers in their worship of lesser ones.[4]

We can deepen the idea by noting that the whole apparatus of idol-craft, along with the priest-craft that surrounds it, is in effect an effort to use and domesticate the god. The god's locus is defined by the locations of his idols, his preferred forms of supplication are dictated by the cultic priests, and what it takes to placate and, in the end, to manipulate the god is set out as a reliable ritualistic stratagem. Instead of God's appearing as the wholly other, the numinous One who transcends anything that we can master by way of our own efforts, he appears as a potential patron, a powerful ally whom we might win over to our side. This is the arena, not of true religion, but of the occult and of magic, be it black or white magic. The self-seeking motives of the human beings involved in such cultic practices are not radically transformed; they are simply projected onto another "spiritual" realm.

There is a massive consensus, across the major religions, that salvation crucially requires overcoming the centripetal force of self-

---

4. This explains why it was not necessarily idolatrous to construct the Ark of the Covenant and adorn it with Golden Angels. God himself had ordained the design; it was not an attempt on the part of the Israelites to contain Divinity. Or if it was, then it was idolatrous.

involvement, in order to orient one's life around reality and the real needs of human beings as such. Given the strength of the centripetal force, it is too easy to invent objects of worship that instead serve as echo chambers for our individual self-worship, or for the collective self-worship of our nation, tribe, or religious group. So the idolater, in declaring fealty to his idolized god, is typically persevering in his own willfulness.

Idolatry is, then, invariably the attempt to evade or ignore the demanding core of true religion: radical self-abandonment to the Divine as manifested in the turn toward others and toward objective reality.

As we shall see, when it comes to idolatrous resistance to the Divine there is a third, oft-used device besides the display of idols and the associated dominance of the priestly caste. This is the religious employment of an occult or hidden other world, and of promises of an afterlife in that world, as a way of soothing the failed aspirations of the unredeemed, and redirecting those aspirations for the all too this-worldly interests of the religion.

To this demonic mix, we may add a fourth device; that of the looming Apocalypse, in which the pent-up frustration of failed idolatrous prophecy about the future course of events is exploded upon the world of the unbelievers.

Idolatry as Servility

The connective tissue that unites the two commandments is the idea that worship, at least in the sense in which idolatry is *perverse* worship, involves an ostensible communication to a putative god of one's fealty to his or her will.[5] In its turn, this helps explain the degrading aspect of idolatrous worship. It is degrading to aspire to live in servitude to another's will, just because the other, real or imagined, is or is supposed to be more powerful than we are. To worship and placate intermediate

---

5. So what is called "ancestor worship," and what normally passes for the adoration of the Virgin Mary in Catholicism, constitute idolatrous worship only if they involve expressions of fealty to the will of the ancestors, or to the will of the Virgin. There may be something wrong with intercessory prayer to the Virgin, but it is not, pace the familiar Protestant motif, *inherently* idolatrous. The Virgin does not have her own agenda; praying to her is like asking someone else to pray for you. And that is typically an expression of the sane view that we need all the help we can get.

spiritual beings is to accept a form of childish servitude to their will. Why should we be servile to the will of certain beings just because they are spiritual beings, and their power is greater than ours? Fear of their power, and lust for the advantages they might confer on us? But we seem to be made for something more than fear of power and lust for advantage. To organize one's life around these motives, to dedicate oneself to the placation of power, is to live a childish and reactive life. Worse than that, to have such an organizing principle is to reinforce in oneself the psychology of a generalized moral duplicity. One will take a different attitude to the powerful and to the lowly, depending on the respective capacity of such persons to confer advantage. That is a reliable sign of being base.

Of course, the Most High might call on us to be guided by his will, but the *legitimacy* of that call does not derive from an awesome power to punish or reward us. The legitimacy of the call can derive only from the fact that the Most High is the true object of our ownmost wills, the very thing we obscurely desire in everything that we desire. (Because he is the Good, as a Platonist might put it.)[6]

In demanding that we be guided by his will, the Most High has to be calling us to express our own most enlightened and authentic willing. That is why the worship of the Highest One is not a form of degrading servitude. The idolaters are *slaves* to their gods, while the worship of the Most High is the embrace of our own truest natures.

It leaves the question of just who *is* worshipping the Most High. It need not be those who have found the most reliable spiritual patron.

THE RHETORIC OF IDOLATROUSNESS

The rhetoric of idolatrousness emerges time and again in the self-definition of Judaism, Christianity, and Islam. Whatever else they disagree

---

6. Compare Iris Murdoch, *The Sovereignty of the Good* (Schocken Books, 1971). See also R. M. Adams's magisterial, in the ordinary secular sense of that term, *Finite and Infinite Goods* (Oxford University Press, 1999), which begins with this identification. Particularly relevant to the present discussion is his very helpful chapter "Idolatry." Another writer whose views on religion and idolatry are usefully considered in this context is Wolfhart Pannenberg; see chaps. 3 and 4 of vol. 1 of his *Systematic Theology* (T & T Clark, 1994).

about, the great monotheistic religions can be found to agree on this: if a religion turns out to be less than a form of engagement with the Most High, then it is idolatrous, and thereby illegitimate, blasphemous, and a waste of our spiritual energies. Of course, it is typically *the others* who fall into these ultimate errors. Once again, the psalmist says,

All the gods of the gentiles are idols. (Psalm 96:5)

And Paul makes a related charge, when he urges the local Christian community to abjure the pagan rituals of Corinth:

Do not be idolaters . . .
    . . . [W]hat they sacrifice, [they sacrifice] to demons, not to God, and I do not want you to become participants with demons. You cannot drink the cup of the Lord and also the cup of demons. You cannot partake of the table of the Lord and of the table of demons. (1 Corinthians 10:7, 21–22)

In 1 Corinthians, the rhetoric of idolatry and consequent demon worship is directed primarily against non-Christian and non-Jewish pagans; but Paul is not averse to deploying his Christ-centered account of idolatry against his fellow Jews. The Epistle to the Romans suggests that the Jews who reject Christ as their long-awaited Messiah are lost in an idolatrous relation to the Torah, expecting that by obedience to the Law they can achieve righteousness as something owed to them by their own efforts. Here, a certain attitude to the Mosaic Law makes *the Law itself* a graven image, a familiar yet fraudulent path to righteousness, which in fact cannot be attained by human effort, but only by God's self-giving grace.

The accusation recurs in Paul's letter to the Christian community in Galatia, who were agitated by the question of whether adherence to the Torah was a condition of being a follower of Christ. So in Galatians 3:17–23 Paul insists that the Torah was not part of God's original promise to Abraham, but was added "four hundred and thirty" years later, a temporary dispensation for the purpose of defining transgression in more determinate detail.

Paul then goes on to impugn the original transmission of the Law as overmediated by way of an angel and another (Moses) who recorded the Law, in contrast to the direct revelation of Christ. Finally, he allows himself to write that the Law is a form of spiritual imprisonment from which Christ freed us.

But before the faith came, we were kept in prison under the Law. (Galatians 3:23)

The rabbis did not lie down in the face of this accusation of idolatrous resistance to the new dispensation. Recall the various denunciations of the Jesus-like figure (figures?) found in the Talmud: that he is the bastard son of a Roman soldier, Panthera (the Panther?), and a whore known as Mary, that he was conceived during menstruation, that he brought magic out of Egypt "by cuttings which he made in his flesh," that he was a great fool *and* a great deceiver, that he sits in boiling excrement in hell—and, worst of all, that he led the Jews into idolatry.[7]

In its turn, the Holy Koran finds the Christian's attitude to Christ to be a manifestation of *al-fitnah* (religious mischief) in the form of *shirk*—an idolatrous displacement of Allah from his position of being without peer.

And they say: The Beneficent God has taken (to Himself) a son. Certainly they have made an abominable assertion. The heavens may almost be rent threat, and the earth cleave asunder, and the mountains fall down in pieces, that they ascribe a son to the Beneficent God. It is not worthy of the Beneficent God that He should take (to Himself) a son. There is no one in the heavens and the earth but will come to the Beneficent God as a servant. (Sura 19:88–93)

And the *takbir*, "Allahu Akbar," the beautiful Muslim cry that sweeps every day across the earth in regular waves, reminds the believer that

7. For a nuanced treatment of the Jewish understanding of Jesus, see Peter Schafer's *Jesus in the Talmud* (Princeton University Press, 2007).

Allah is greater, inter alia greater than those objects of worship that amaze the infidels.

Thus, in each of the three monotheisms, we find the common idea of idolatry as *alien* belief and worship, with the immediate consequence that *we* could not be the idolaters. After all, the founders of *our* religion *were* addressed by the Highest One, and *our* form of worship of him is only what he commanded, and where it is not that, surely it is only a legitimate extension of what he commanded. How, then, could it be possible that *we* are the idolaters?

Such are the reflex comforts of a narrow ethnocentrism. In fact, the rhetoric of idolatry cannot be so comfortably contained, so that it will always turn out that it is *the others* who are the idolaters. For the inner logic of the charge of idolatry is to interrogate worship of all kinds, both as to the object of worship ("Is it the Highest One who is here venerated?") and as to the manner of worship ("Is this a fitting way to venerate the Highest One?").

As for the object of worship, the rhetoric of idolatry serves to intensify awareness of the transcendence of the true God, thereby encouraging a *retroactive* skepticism as to whether it was indeed the true God who appeared in the manifestations that were formative of one's own religion. As to the manner of worship, one may find in one's own religious practice a growing fixation on the outer ritual forms, rather than the genuine inner condition, with a resulting occlusion of the true God. Even if one's religion began with the revelation of the Highest One, that revelation is too easily appropriated by unredeemed worldly interests projected onto the revelation, often by the priestly brokers of the religion.

By definition, one's own worship cannot be *alien*, but it can be, or become, perverse.[8]

---

8. Compare Paul Tillich, *Systematic Theology*, vol. 1 (University of Chicago Press, 1951), 216.

Holiness cannot become actual except through holy "objects." But holy objects are not holy in and of themselves. They are holy only by negating themselves in pointing to the divine of which they are mediums. If they establish themselves as holy they become demonic. . . . This happens continually in the actual life of most religions. The representations of man's ultimate concern—holy objects—tend to become his ultimate concern. They are transformed into idols. Holiness provokes idolatry. (As quoted in Adams, *Finite and Infinite Goods*, 210–11)

The Same God?

Could it be that the great monotheistic religions, Judaism, Christianity, and Islam, as they stand now, are idolatrous, and so forms of resistance to the Divine? Many will find that an impious, and therefore an evil, thought. And yet it is right alongside a thought that each one of the great monotheistic religious has, from time to time, harbored about the other two. That is evident in the carefulness and regularity with which this second thought has to be put down.

Pope Benedict's address at Regensburg University, one day after the fifth anniversary of the September 11 atrocity, produced outrage in the Muslim world. There it was widely regarded as a not-so-veiled attack on Islam as a religion that condoned violence perpetrated in its name. As a result, an Australian nun and her bodyguard were killed in Somalia; Morocco recalled its ambassador from the Vatican; and Sheikh Hassan Malin of Somalia's Supreme Islamic Council went so far as to direct his fellow Muslims to assassinate the pope, saying,

> Wherever you are, [you must] hunt down the pope for his barbaric statements, as you have pursued Salman Rushdie, the enemy of Allah who offended our religion. Whoever offends our Prophet Muhammad should be killed on the spot by the nearest Muslim.[9]

The Army of the Pure in Pakistan followed suit, issuing a fatwa ordering the Muslim community to eliminate Pope Benedict for his blasphemous remarks about the Prophet. Even Al Qaeda found it necessary to say something against the Holy Father.

Benedict, a man whose academic theology is condemned by so-called traditionalist Catholics precisely because of its reasoned openness to other religions, was clearly blindsided by the reaction. He immediately moved to reassure Muslim leaders, reiterating the Catholic Church's position on Islam by invoking *Nostra Aetate* (In Our Time),

---

I take it that in these remarks "object" is not restricted to relics, images, and icons. It stands for a portmanteau category that includes sacraments, sacred texts, and churches as well.

9. "Somali Cleric Calls for Pope's Death," *The Age*, September 17, 2006.

a 1965 document from the Second Vatican Council, particularly this passage:

> The Church looks upon Muslims with respect. They worship the one God, living and subsistent, merciful and almighty, creator of heaven and earth, who has spoken to humanity and to whose decrees, even the hidden ones, they seek to submit themselves whole-heartedly, just as Abraham, to whom the Islamic faith readily relates itself, submitted to God.

The reference to Abraham is a crucial part of the conciliatory gesture. For Jews, Christians, and Muslims all rejoice under the title of "Children of Abraham." Each can identify the others as tracing their religion to a god's encounter with Abraham. Yes; but do they, as *Nostra Aetate* assumes, really take it to be *the same god*? Is the Holy Trinity Allah? Is Yahweh the Holy Trinity? Is Yahweh Allah? And just how extensive are these "hidden decrees," which *Nostra Aetate* suggests Islam knows only *as hidden*, whereas the Magisterium knows them explicitly?

These questions as to the identity of the gods present themselves differently to atheists than they do to believers. Atheists will suppose that no divine being ever addressed mankind, and so they are likely to see in the formative experiences of the major religions nothing better than religious hallucinations, perhaps enhanced by power-seeking doctrine-mongers. Given this deflationary treatment of religious experience, there is no good way to answer the question "Is it the same God?" beyond making a comparison between the relevant core conceptions of God. When we investigate the respective core conceptions of the Abrahamic religions, we do find some overlap, but also, profound differences. For example, on any close inspection, Yahweh and God the Father seem to be quite dissimilar personalities, as dissimilar, you might say, as Tony Soprano and Mr. Rogers. (At least that is how it seems until the likes of Matthew 25.)

It is different for a believer in one or another of the Abrahamic religions; for a believer, the question of the same God reduces to a question of Who appeared to whom. Was it Allah who addressed Abraham, as many Muslims themselves believe? If so, then it must be said that in his dealings with Abraham, Allah was being quite careful with the truth about himself; his revelation was at best slowly parceled out over time, with much of his real preferences about how he should be conceived of, and worshipped, being held back. Accordingly, there must have been much that was illusory and occluded in Abraham's experience and conception of the Being, namely, Allah, who on this hypothesis appeared to him.

Here, by identifying Yahweh and Allah, one may, in principle, make an accommodation of the one religion to the other; but obviously it is an accommodation that is more pleasing to Islam than to Judaism.

Moreover, as the sura quoted above suggests, it is much more difficult to make a corresponding accommodation between Islam and Christianity. Muslims *should* be very leery of extending the same conciliatory gesture as that extended to them by *Nostra Aetate*. Christians do appear to worship Christ, the second person of the Trinity, and worship him as such. By way of several suras like the one quoted above, the Holy Koran makes it clear that it would be abominable to assert that Christ (or even the Father) is Allah. It would "rend the heavens and cleave the earth" to thus suppose that Allah was a member of a Trinity of Equal Divine Persons. So good Muslims must say that the worship of Christ is simply and straightforwardly *shirk*—an idolatrous substitution of something other than Allah for Allah—and therefore represents the serious kind of religious mischief that, as another Koranic passage tells us, "is worse than murder."

There is a purified form of Christian worship that escapes this argument that Christianity is inherently *shirk*. A Christian himself might admit that strictly speaking it is idolatrous to worship Christ, the second person of the Blessed Trinity, as such. Compare the (outside of Pentecostalism, surprisingly neglected) cult of worship of the Holy Spirit, the third person of the Blessed Trinity. That could be made to seem idolatrous, even to some Christians. They might be led to ask: Why is this person being put in the place of the Holy Trinity? In that way, they might be led to the idea that the proper object of worship, even in Christianity, is neither the Son, nor the Father, nor the Holy Spirit. It is the One Holy Trinity, which incorporates these three persons.

However, *actual* Christians do seem to declare fealty not only to the Son, but also to the Father, as in the Lord's Prayer, which is straightforwardly addressed to the Father, and which concludes, "For *thine* is the

Kingdom and the Power and the Glory, world without end, Amen."
But again, it might be said that all this is just one way of declaring
fealty to the Triune God. Christians who adopt this view may then take
Muslims to be worshipping the Triune God, under the name of "Allah."
It is just that Muslims fail to recognize the Trinitarian complexity in
the inner personality of God.

From the point of view of Islam, that would be simply another af-
front. The Holy Koran does not leave the inner personality of God
open. It is itself *shirk* to suppose that Allah consists of three persons.
Even if Christians insist that the true and only object of their worship
is the Holy Trinity, it will follow from the Muslim point of view that
either Christians worship something distinct from Allah, in which case
they are idolaters, or they have a blasphemous conception of the inner
personality of Allah, which manifests itself in the idolatrous cults of the
Father and the Son.

Many good Muslims may have the grace not to say all this to their
Christian friends, or they may prevaricate when it is said; *but it is the
logic of their faith.* It is yet another expression of the radical exclusivity
of Islam's monotheism.

The Pharisees' Problem with Jesus

Yahweh's ban on graven images is naturally understood as a ban on the
"living" idols of the Egyptian and Canaanite cults. Priests of those cults
sometimes manipulated the limbs and faces of the cultic statues, and
on high and holy days spoke through them to create the impression of
living idols, inhabited by the gods they represented. Correspondingly,
the Jewish mockery of those idols consists of describing them as lifeless
or dead, as in Psalm 115:5–8:

> Their idols are silver and gold, the work of men's hands.
> They have mouths, but they speak not: eyes have they, but they
> see not:
> They have ears, but they hear not: noses have they, but they
> smell not:

They have hands, but they handle not: feet have they, but they walk not: neither speak they through their throat.

The very charge that the embodiments of the gods are in reality lifeless opens up a theological space to be filled. A living being might confound this whole tradition of the rejection of "living" idols by declaring *himself* to be the embodiment of the Highest One. This would be the ultimate idolatrous provocation, and it would mark an irredeemable break with the inner self-conception of Judaism, and of its own privileged historical relation to the Highest One.

In the eighth chapter of the Gospel of John, Jesus delivers just this ultimate provocation to the Pharisees. Declaring himself to be sent by the Father, he seems to appropriate for himself the very nature of the Highest One.[10]

"Very truly I tell you," Jesus answered, "before Abraham was born, *I am*!" At this, they picked up stones to stone him. (John 8:58)

Of course they did; how else could they be expected to act? Even if this happened, the Christian charge of attempted deicide is, of course, completely misplaced; for in attempting to stone Jesus, the Pharisees were trying to preserve the holy dignity of the Highest One.

Could *We* Be Idolaters?

The extramural charges of idolatry cannot be so easily put to rest by way of facile and condescending identifications of the objects of worship of the major monotheisms. What, then, of the intramural charges of idolatry?

The three great monotheistic religions are crucially religions of revelation, and of books which describe that revelation, and, in the case

---

10. Is Jesus here appropriating the tetragrammaton, the divine name revealed to Moses, for himself? Harold Bloom, against the informed convictions of leading mainstream New Testament scholars, argues that he is. See Bloom, *Jesus and Yahweh: The Names Divine* (Penguin USA, 2005), 75–78.

of Islam, of a book, the Holy Koran, which ostensibly *constitutes* that revelation. A revelation, in this sense, is nothing less than God himself addressing humanity, so each of the three religions represents itself as beginning with God's addressing certain specific human beings.

It is also part of the self-definition of the major monotheistic religions to oppose idolatry, for in doing that, they define themselves as religions in which the Highest One reveals himself.

It follows that if any of the major monotheistic religions are in any sense authentic, then the Highest One must have *addressed* some human being such as Abraham, Moses, or Muhammad. (In that last case, the Highest One must have addressed Muhammad through the agency of his messenger the angel Gabriel, as Islam claims.) And in the case of Christianity, it must be that Jesus was in some very special way the embodiment of the Highest One, so that his addressing those around him was ipso facto the Highest One addressing them.

Otherwise, by their own lights, the major monotheistic religions began as frauds—frauds in which something less than the Highest One, something real or merely apparent, presented itself as the Highest One.

The second possibility, mere appearance, is less sinister. For it involves the elaboration of a hallucination or an illusion, or in the best case a natural religious experience, in tendentious metaphysical and cultic directions.

For reasons of method we must also keep in mind the first, more sinister possibility, emphasized by Marcion and the Gnostics: that of an intermediate spiritual being passing itself off as the Highest One. (Though in Marcion's view, Yahweh, before deceiving others, had taken the elementary precaution of deceiving himself as to his own primacy.) A negative verdict on the question as to whether the foundational religious experiences of a given religion were a presentation or a manifestation of the Highest One does not entail that those experiences were illusory or hallucinatory. To arrive at that conclusion, one would have to rule out other, lesser gods, and even demons, as the objects of the experiences. And how might we do that?

Rather than expend energy on that task, we should proceed "phenomenologically." We should take the ostensible revelation or manifestation on its own terms and ask: If this foundational religious experience *were* a veridical experience, would it be the revelation or manifestation of the Highest One?

This deserves to be called a "phenomenological" approach because it brackets the question of existence and focuses on the content of the foundational revelations, that is, on what would be the case if the ostensible revelation *were* veridical. The approach treats the respective ostensible, or "intentional," objects of the supposedly revelatory experiences as in part constitutive of those very experiences, whether those objects exist or not. Hence we express no opinion *as to the existence* of the ostensible spiritual beings who seemed in those experiences of revelation to be addressing this or that human being. We simply do not enter into the question of whether Yahweh, or the Father, or Allah, exists. Likewise, we do not take issue with the historicity of the Gospels. We take the foundational religious experiences *as they present to their subjects*. We then look at the implied character of the putative spiritual beings who ostensibly appear in these experiences.

Now it lies within the natural capacities of human beings to determine something of the character of another by his mode of address, what he says, which actions he favors, and which he rejects. Call this the inference from behavior to character. Throughout our evolutionary history we were selected (certainly by evolution, and perhaps by the Creator, by means of evolution) partly on the basis of being better and not worse at the inference from behavior to character. As a result, we are rather good at that inference. And so one proper method in approaching the various religions is to take at face value their descriptions of the primary revelations of God *to* this or that human being or *in* this or that human being, and then ask: Do we see here the character of the Highest One?

It is a question worth asking only if we have some sort of understanding of the nature or character of the Highest One. So a presupposition of our method is that we do have some understanding in this area: minimally a partial understanding that might come from a widespread, if underdeveloped, religious sense of things, and the refinement of that sense by reflection, including reflection on the history of religion. This antecedent religious sense of things may be in some respects compared to the musical sense. The musical sense reveals a domain, with respect to which some are simply deaf. There is a corresponding spiritual "tone deafness," found even in certain writers on religion. And there also must be the religious counterpart of really deficient musical training. And of kitsch musical taste.

Our antecedent knowledge of the Highest One may mostly consist of negative propositions concerning the character of the Highest One. This knowledge is "antecedent" knowledge in that it is not derived from specific revelations; it is potentially available independently of those revelations. Any serious engagement with our questions should proceed on minimal assumptions about the deliverances of the antecedent religious sense. It will be too much to assume that we have naturally, and independently of any revelation of the Highest One, any rich positive knowledge of the intrinsic character of the Highest One.

Still, to be flat-footed about it for a moment, we do know of the Highest One that there could *not* be one Higher, for if there could be, then that (actual or possible being) would be a more proper object of love, fealty, and worship. We also know that the Highest One could *not* have evil intent, nor a contempt for the truth. All this is only negative knowledge of the character of the Highest One, and we shall look to see how far we can proceed in the examination of religion without supposing that the antecedent religious sense of things provides much more than such negative knowledge of the Highest One.

So our question is: Does the phenomenology of the foundational experiences of this or that version of monotheism display the character of the Highest One? And, collaterally, how should a religion cope with the discovery that it has committed its adherents to a lesser one?

Chapter 3

Supernaturalism and Scientism

SCIENTISM AND SUPERSTITION

As an approach to the monotheistic religions, the phenomenological method and the question of character contrast with the blanket criticism of religion as a morass of obsolete belief systems that have been shown, by the accumulation of scientific discoveries, to be irrational. Looking at religion through the lens of idolatry may simply preempt such criticism, and preempt it *from within the religious point of view itself.* After idolatry is purged, not every "religion" will actually be a religion, and little in the way of "religious doctrine" will be religious. Few will have actually had a religion, as opposed to a simulacrum of one.[1] And the allegedly obsolete belief systems may well have been idolatrous before they were provably false. So once the idolatrous elements are removed, there may be little for science to contradict.

The recent perfervid attacks on "religion" and "God" by Sam Harris, Richard Dawkins, and Christopher Hitchens exhibit a tendency to de-

---

1. This kind of remark will seem incoherent to those writers like Kent Greenawalt who with some plausibility suppose that "religion" is a family resemblance term whose criteria of application are in part drawn from the three monotheisms themselves. Wittgenstein's paradigm of a family resemblance term is "game." There is, Wittgenstein supposed, no underlying essence of games; there is only a variety of crisscrossing similarities holding together the family of games. From the point of view of an officially secular sociology of religion there may appear to be no other option than Greenawalt's, namely, to make it more or less a trivial fact that the cults of Yahweh, of the Father, and of Allah are religions. But for a believer in the Highest One, "religion" is semantically more like "gold" than like "game." (Compare Barth, *Church Dogmatics.*) Whereas a good simulacrum of a game *is* a game, a good simulacrum of gold may be only fool's gold. For a believer in the Highest One, a false religion is more like false or "fool's" gold than like a false proposition, which is after all still a proposition. For such a person, a religion is something that encourages an appropriate life-orientation toward the Highest One. It will then be very hard to have a religion, properly so speaking. There will not be a lot of religion around.

Perhaps "gold" is too much. A better analogy for "religion" is "healer"; a purveyor of snake oil is not a healer, even if he has all the external apparatus and reputation of one. The Constitution *would* be a "suicide pact" if it invalidated laws that turned on the distinction between a healer and a mere simulacrum of one.

generate into set pieces in which scientism does battle with superstition, and (surprise, surprise) it is scientism that emerges as the unscathed victor.[2] The set pieces—the horrors of sectarian violence; evolution versus creationism; preventable evil versus God's omnipotence and benevolence; the extreme improbability, perhaps even incoherence, of miraculous violations of natural law, and so on and so forth—do have certain familiar charms. But they are largely the quickly fading charms of undergraduate atheism. The set pieces seem to have lasting appeal only to those who manage to combine spiritual tone deafness with a naive view of scientific method.

The atheism of Dawkins and Hitchens bids fair to be called "undergraduate" atheism, for several reasons. First, decades ago, when these men were undergraduates, atheism had triumphantly won the day, at least in their culture circles, and it was terribly bad form to be a believer. This stands in stark contrast to the way things are now in the United States, where it recently seemed extraordinary, even courageous, for a newly inaugurated president to publicly recognize the mere existence of unbelievers among the citizenry. So one can readily understand why Dawkins and Hitchens would feel that if only the old arguments were repeated *over and over again*, the halcyon days might return. Sam Harris, on the other hand, *is* an undergraduate, or was one a few years ago, and so is able to present the old considerations with a youthful brio, as if he himself had invented them.

Second, it is clear that each of these polemicists is capable of writing what he does only by having neglected the relevant *postgraduate* texts: in particular Immanuel Kant's *Religion within the Limits of Reason Alone* and Baruch Spinoza's *Ethics,* along with his *Theological-Political Treatise.* Christopher Hitchens, in a recent debate with the Reverend Al Sharpton, and on *The Daily Show,* and again in an interview with Lou Dobbs, went so far as to invoke Spinoza as one of his atheistic heroes. Hitchens, a man who is not without philosophical training, would have done better to have actually read Spinoza, the "God-obsessed man"

---

2. Sam Harris, *The End of Faith* (Norton, 2004); Richard Dawkins, *The God Delusion* (Houghton Muffin, 2006); Christopher Hitchens, *God Is Not Great: How Religion Poisons Everything* (Hachette Book Group, 2007).

who nonetheless developed an antisupernaturalist account of scripture and of salvation. Spinoza, recall, was a thoroughgoing rationalist, who nonetheless regarded Christ as a, and perhaps *the*, savior.[3] Dawkins, if anything, is even more innocent of Spinoza's soteriology. He refers to Spinoza as a pantheist, and calls pantheism "atheism sexed-up," thereby implying that Spinoza's view was just atheism sexed-up.[4] That makes the CliffsNotes version of Spinoza look like Harry Austryn Wolfson.

The "undergraduate" atheists, if we may call them that without reflecting adversely on actual undergraduates, uncritically share a defective premise with their secret fundamentalist allies, namely, that religion is essentially supernaturalist, and that those who deny this have somehow gone soft or are evading the real commitments of religion. Only in this way can the undergraduate atheists slap down their trump card of Darwinism's old victory over Creationism as if it were a card strong enough to discredit religion, or God, as such. There is no shame in reminding us of that old victory; the shame is in packaging the victory as something it is not. There is an important sense in which real religion never comes into view in these three authors. (Did they meet in a back room with the fundamentalists, long ago, to agree to collaborate in the task of obscuring real religion?)

As we shall see, the very ideas of religion as essentially supernaturalist, and of God as essentially a supernatural being, are idolatrous conceptions. The idolatrous religions degrade their putative experience of Divinity by entirely wedding it to the passing and adventitious worldviews of their founding fathers. So the hard work of reexpressing the experience of Divinity within a more plausible worldview does not get done, because elements of the outdated worldview have come to provide crucial secondary compensations for those who would use their religion as a venue for spiritual materialism. But this, at least in principle, allows for other, less idolatrous, expressions of that experience. And

---

3. So Spinoza writes at i, 24 in the *Theological-Political Treatise*: "A man who can by pure intuition comprehend ideas which are neither contained in nor deducible from the foundations of our natural knowledge, must necessarily possess a mind far superior to those of his fellow men, nor do I believe that any have been so endowed save Christ. To Him the ordinances of God leading men to salvation were revealed directly without words or visions . . . Christ communed with God, mind to mind."

4. Dawkins, *The God Delusion*, chap. 1.

this demand, for religion without idolatry, or, more realistically, for a *less* idolatrous religion, is internal to monotheism itself.

In contrast to this, the undergraduate atheists build superstition and supernaturalism into the very meaning of "religion," and so by mere semantic artifice occlude the very possibility of religion without idolatry, the only good candidate to be real religion. Compare making the common and unquestioned racism of the American Founding Fathers an essential feature of the intent behind the Constitution, and then finding, as a result, that the Voting Rights Act is unconstitutional. Are we to be told that we have now gone soft on the real commitments of the Constitution, as expressed, say, in the decision in *Dred Scott*?

Rather than gerrymandering the terminology, one way or another, we should explore the extent of a legitimate naturalism, so as to better understand both naturalism itself and the way in which a religion can be consistent with naturalism. No doubt our religions are idolatrous forms of resistance to the Divine, for they are in part expressions of a compromise with the historical conditions of our spiritual materialism, the projections of our unredeemed longings onto a supposed spiritual realm. But are those religions *essentially* idolatrous? Can their spiritual message survive the purging of their supernaturalist and superstitious elements? That is not a question to be settled by nominal definition, or by a mere choice of terminology.

Supernaturalism

Supernaturalism is belief in invisible spiritual agencies whose putative interventions would violate the laws of nature, at least as those laws are presently understood. In this sense of supernaturalism, tied as it is to our present understanding of the laws of nature, certain beliefs may *become* supernaturalist thanks to our developing understanding of just how nature works. So in this sense, the sacred texts of the three monotheisms are full of supernaturalism.

Take the authors of the Gospels. "Mark," whoever that enigmatic and complex person was, clearly believes that the natural realm, the world that he moves around in, the world that exhausts all the places he could in principle get to by traveling in the ordinary sense, is a world of magic, spirits, demons, possession, miraculous healing, transubstantiation of materials, direct intentional action at a distance, and blessing and election by a preeminent god (is it Yahweh?) who is intermittently active in that world.

What are we to make of this essentially mantic worldview?

If, in a spirit of lazy anachronism, we took this ancient worldview as a competitor to current science, then it would be bad science. And two thousand years from now, many aspects of our worldview will simply appear to be bad science too. But how does that sort of fact, the fact of scientific progress, engage with the ethical and spiritual aspirations that we might now express within our present worldview? Isn't the only decent hope that those aspirations are not essentially tied to our confusions about nature and our place in it? What else can we do?

Suppose someone says: Here is my best attempt to bring into reflective equilibrium all I know about the world from science and philosophy, and given this picture of reality, here is an identification of the Highest One, and an account of how he or it could exert a salvific influence on us. And suppose the science and philosophy turns out subsequently to be discovered to be wrong in respects crucial to the identification of the Highest One and his salvific influence. That is unfortunate, but it is to be expected. We are fallible creatures, and the conceptual frame within which we express our ethical and spiritual aspirations, the only frame within which the Highest One could possibly address us,[5] is an evolving and fallible one. There can be radical transformations in the frame, say as between the worldviews of the ancient Near East and the worldview of the typical devoted reader of *Nature* or *Scientific American*, or as between that second "scientifically informed" worldview and the science of the forty-first century. But such radical transformations in the frame leave open the question of whether the salvific idea of the Highest One can still find an authentic expression in the new and better understanding of reality. This question, one of the few real questions behind all the popular bumf that goes under the heading of "science versus religion," is a question we cannot answer simply by observing that the frame has radically changed, and that we now have a better understanding of many aspects of reality.

---

5. For a defense of this, see the remarks below about religious experience and *seeing as*.

It may be, for example, something of an open and, if open, very hard question as to how much of what is offered as revelatory in the Gospel of Mark is *essentially* tied to the author's quite false conception of how the natural realm works, especially if that Gospel is left unmolested by the additions of false endings and other, later interpolations. At one level, and I am very far from saying that this is all that there is in it,[6] Mark's narrative is a most extraordinary form of spiritual argument from an exemplary case.

"A man, a wonder-worker and an author of dark sayings, came and proclaimed the Reign of God; his followers saw him as the promised Messiah of Israel, and perhaps he had the power and presence to free Israel from the Roman yoke. But he turned away from all that because of his utter self-abandonment to the will of God. He continued to proclaim the Reign of God in the face of a stony and uncomprehending reception. This lead to his torture, to humiliation, to desertion by his followers, and to his agonizing and despairing death at the hands of the legitimate religious and political powers. Take heed of that example in your own much simpler and humbler case!"

Recall that although Mark has Jesus being elected by the voice from the heavens and has him endowed with the most extraordinary powers (as would befit a potential messiah), Mark in the original has no Virgin Birth, no glorious return from the dead, no liftoff from the Mount of Olives, and certainly no doctrine of Christ's atonement for our sins, but only—in the original ending—the women confronting the empty tomb, and then confusion, deflation, and fear: reactions utterly consistent with Mark's ruthless chronicle of the *systematic* misunderstanding of Christ exhibited by his hapless disciples (excepting perhaps the young man in the white robe).[7] Here are the last words of the unaugmented Gospel of Mark:

Trembling and bewildered, the women went out and fled from the tomb. They said nothing to anyone, because they were afraid. (Mark 16:8)

6. For example, we must also take account of passages like "After I am raised up, I will go before you to Galilee" (14:28) and the echo of this at 16:7.

7. For more on Mark's intentions, see the papers collected by Beverly Roberts Gaventa and Patrick D. Miller in *The Ending of Mark and the Ends of God* (Westminster John Knox, 2005),

At this level of the narrative, the level of the argument from the exemplary case, there is no essential tie between the salvific message of Mark's Gospel—the Reign of God has come, what it demands of you will make no sense in worldly terms, yet even so your salvation lies in abandonment to the will of God—and the confusions about the natural realm shared by Mark and his contemporaries.

That changes when a particular salvific idea from a particular sect within Judaism, namely, the Pharisaical idea of personal resurrection, is applied to Christ, so that we get the mystical theology of Christ Dead, Christ Bodily Risen, Christ to Come Again in Compensating Glory at the Final Judgment of the Living and the Dead. These ideas, at least in the form in which the Pharisee Paul held them, cannot be expressed within a legitimate naturalism.[8]

Legitimate Naturalism

Legitimate naturalism arises out of proper respect for the methods and achievements of science. Science is first and foremost a complex and open-ended collection of ways of finding out about the world. What these methods of inquiry have in common is a matter of significant philosophical dispute, but several similarities (or are they just family resemblances?) seem too obvious to neglect. There is the attractive bias of resolving disputes by turning to repeatable, and so intersubjectively available, observations. Then there is the admirable critical habit of using such observations to refine and refute hypotheses about the natural realm, and the larger theories in which such hypotheses are embedded. These theories are intended to model their respective domains of inquiry, and these models suggest new hypotheses, and ways of controlling experimental and observation settings, so as to test the new hypothesis. A contender for the title of "best theory" in a given domain must not only save the phenomena proper to its domain; it is also under considerable pressure to mesh with the best theories in other domains,

---

particularly the lead essay by Donald Juel. Does the original ending of Mark with its empty tomb present a question to the reader as to just what the promised *anastasis* or rising up consists in?

8. For detailed argument to this effect, see *Surviving Death* (Princeton University Press, 2009).

so that a unified, or at least not irredeemably conflicted, picture of reality emerges.

It would be naive not to add to this conception of science as a form of theoretical understanding a recognition of the essentially technological orientation of much of science; the aim is to produce not just theories but also more useful devices, and not only devices useful at large, but devices, techniques, experimental equipment, and methods useful within the special sciences themselves. Partly owing to the enormously distorting impact of funding by the military-industrial complex during the Cold War, science has become more and more the handmaiden of technology, and is now driven by an agenda that in significant degree makes the technological potential of a discovery the hallmark of its intellectual significance.

Religion, for its part, is a complex and open-ended collection of cultic practices from which the practitioners derive, or hope to derive, "existential strength," that is, a deepened capacity to deal with the manifest, large-scale structural defects of human life.[9] To say that is not to indulge in noncognitivism about religion, the reductive treatment of religion as a mere practice with a set of associated virtues. The development of existential strength will involve believing in other things and other people, and may include believing in God; and that will involve associated belief in many distinctive propositions. But it is just unskillful to develop existential strength by believing propositions that encroach on the domain of science, thereby making one's path to salvation hostage to future scientific discoveries. And the Highest One could not ask this of us.

The very idea of a refutation of religion by science is thus a misplaced generality. It would have to involve the singular scientific result that there is no authentic source of existential strength. Which subfields of science are working on that question, and with what methods?

Collaterally, once we investigate the details of actual religions, the idea of a generic conflict between religion and science seems an all-too-

9. The concept of religion used here is akin to the family resemblance concept of religion that is understandably deployed by a secular sociology of religion. On the more demanding use of "religion" outlined in the first footnote in this chapter, any clash between religion and science will be a clash between appropriate worship of the Highest One and the true description of nature. But that seems impossible, since the Highest One cannot require that we believe or act on falsehoods.

simple theme. Take Advaita Vedanta, or Theravada Buddhism, or Zen; they say nothing at odds with evolutionary biology, so is it cosmology or chemistry or botany or mathematics with which they are in essential conflict? What scientific falsehoods can we discover in the theological core of Confucianism? Or in that of Taoism?

Nor is monotheism inherently in conflict with "science." In showing this, we need not explore the demanding doctrines of Kant and Ernst Troeltsch, nor even those of Hermann Cohen, who regarded it as a sign of true Judaism that there could be no such question about conflict with science.[10] It is simpler. What experimental results are the Unitarians committed to denying? Or consider the Bahá'ís, who assert as a central tenet of their religion the interanimating harmony of religion and science, comparing them to the two wings of a bird, each essential if the bird is to take to the air. The Bahá'ís explicitly reject as superstitious any religious teachings that are at odds with the scientific revelation of God's truth.

Surely the Bahá'ís have something here; science ought to be regarded as the close friend of true theology, for it is enormously helpful in ridding religion of superstition. For the Highest One cannot be a deceiver, and so any material falsehood in his ostensible message must be due to human accretion, or deception by intermediate powers. It is clear, and utterly unsurprising, that the monotheisms of the ancient Near East were often tempted into collaborating with the limited world pictures of their day, expressing even their most genuine religious insights in these now-refuted terms. Who could deny, for example, that it is something of an insult to the Highest One to have his Son depicted as returning to him by lifting off from the Mount of Olives, as if the Highest One were located at some distance from the Earth? What, after all, was the flight plan governing the Ascension?

Irritation at the way in which genuine religious insight is obscured by such obsolete world pictures is one thing. The insinuation of a "Godless" metaphysical picture induced by scientism is another. When the argument from the one to the other proceeds simply by a definition that confuses the historical, and supernaturalist, expression of a religion

---

10. See, for example, Hermann Cohen's essential *Ethics of Maimonides*, now translated with a commentary by Almut Sh. Bruckstein (University of Wisconsin Press, 2002).

with its salvific core, we can be sure that we are not in the presence of a spirit of intellectual seriousness.

Richard Dawkins, thanks to this kind of carelessness, has made a considerable journalistic reputation as a hotshot refuter of religion. Even as early as 1992, in a debate with the then archbishop of York, Dr. John Habgood, at the Edinburgh Science Festival, Dawkins offered this:

> You can't escape the scientific implications of religion. A universe with a God would look quite different from a universe without one. A physics, a biology where there is a God is bound to look different. So the most basic claims of religion *are* scientific. Religion *is* a scientific theory.

It isn't. Or at least it isn't unless we restrict "religion" to what is idolatrous or spiritually materialistic, and so already defective as a religion. Argumentatively, Dawkins's bald identification is impotent, since we can give him the word he is so keen to kidnap, and all the substantive theological and philosophical issues will still remain.

Scientism versus Science

The charge of "scientism" is best understood as the accusation that a certain use of the scientific world picture, particularly a metaphysical use in which it is presented as an exhaustive inventory of reality, depends upon forgetting the abstractive preconditions of scientific modeling. Various domains are amenable to scientific understanding because they can be modeled by way of a precise vocabulary, often the vocabulary of mathematics. The vocabulary and the models then provide testable predictions, and experimental investigation involves a set of routines whose outcomes are typically agreed upon by the practitioners of the science in question. So a growing consensus develops as to the nature of various aspects of reality.

This is genuine progress in understanding the world, but, like every other real advance, it comes at a price. The scientific method essentially involves redescription of the phenomena and modeling of the phenomena. In these two ways, among others, less tractable aspects of reality are rightly ignored. Scientism, the idea that the basic science, physics, will provide an exhaustive inventory of what there is, involves forgetting this strategically important ignoring. The things we abstracted away from in our mathematical descriptions and models are no less real because of their relative intractability. The idea that this selective focus will cost us nothing in our knowledge of reality—therein lies the methodological naïveté of scientism.

What harm is there in the naïveté? What is actually left out of the resultant inventory? Well, for one, the very intelligibility of things, which makes science possible. Scientism's way with the intelligibility of things has been to treat it as a subjective phenomenon, and then to shunt it off to the side as a research program titled "the problem of consciousness." The research program has been degenerating (in Imre Lakatos's technical sense of yielding less and less, despite more and more effort)[11] ever since certain Australian philosophers revived philosophical materialism in the sixties. Moreover, as will emerge below, the very idea of "the problem of consciousness" depends on a misconception of consciousness itself.

As well as treating intelligibility as a merely subjective phenomenon, scientism also represents a failure to think through the ontological implications of the objectivity of reason, and the objectivity of epistemic norms, on which science essentially relies. How can reasons be objective, if all that exists is space-time and its wholly material occupants?[12]

In these two ways, scientism cannot account for the fundamental preconditions of the sciences themselves.

Scientism aside, science may properly aspire to a certain kind of *causal* completeness in its modeling of reality, and as this detailed causal knowledge becomes widespread, only a deep duplicity of mind will allow continued adherence to ancient Near Eastern world pictures. Again, this means that so far from there being a deep opposition between something called "science" and something called "religion," sci-

11. Imre Lakatos, *The Methodology of Scientific Research Programmes*, vol. 1 of *Philosophical Papers* (Cambridge University Press, 1977).

12. Of course, philosophers have had an enormous amount to say about this, and perhaps the best account on the other side would be an adaptation of Peter Railton's naturalistic moral realism to the case of epistemic norms. See his "Moral Realism," *Philosophical Review* 85 (1986).

ence can be a driving force in divesting religion of superstition. In this way it happens to serve the deeper interests of theology. The Bahá'ís are right: because the Highest One cannot be a deceiver, the bird's two wings must be made for each other.

In particular, science is enormously helpful in the battle against divination, occultism, and other forms of spiritual materialism that look to the god or gods for advantageous interventions in ordinary life, and so treat the spiritual domain as just another realm in which the lust for advantage may be indulged.

So, even from the side of religion, the scientific ambition of modeling reality in a way that is causally complete and self-contained should be respected and encouraged. The ambition can be explained in different ways. It might be understood as the attempt to find both a vocabulary that subsumes all events, and a set of natural laws cast in that vocabulary, so that all causation between events can be seen to be natural rather than supernatural, that is, to follow from, or be made probable by, the laws of nature and the antecedent conditions of the caused events.

Perhaps reduction of all sciences to a basic science like physics by way of bridging laws between the sciences is no longer a viable hope. But there remains the appealing aspiration to find a precise and sufficiently general vocabulary in which any event or change can in principle be described, and described in such a way that it can then be brought under the aegis of the "laws of nature." That idea is easier to explain if we think of such laws as captured by statements with the logical form of universal generalizations that connect antecedent event-types with consequent event-types with a given probability. Then any event, under its respective privileged description, will be expected to flow with a certain probability from previous events, as a matter of natural law. So if one event is found to immediately cause another, then, given redescriptions of the events in the privileged vocabulary, there will be a certain sort of derivation of that singular causal connection from statements of law.

That is, roughly, how the philosopher Donald Davidson expressed the idea that a basic science might provide a causally complete model of reality. Davidson called this expression of the idea "the nomological character of causation."[13] He regarded the nomological (or law-governed) character of causation to be a matter of actual fact rather than merely the expression of a sound methodological principle to the effect that we should look for the laws and the privileged descriptions. Even so, there is *something* to be said for Davidson's transition from the methodological principle to the corresponding metaphysical hypothesis, namely, the widespread explanatory and predictive success that comes from following the principle.

Davidson supposed that the privileged universal vocabulary was that of some future extension of modern physics. Perhaps this is a good way to give content to the idea that physics is the *basic* science of nature. Yet once that status is granted to physics, the idea of redescribing all activities, achievements, and accomplishments in the vocabulary of physics begins to seem a trifle bizarre. For activities, achievements, and accomplishments have their own manifest form, which it is precisely the business of physics to abstract away from in the name of providing clear quantitative models of the underlying transactions involved. No one should think that an ordinary description of the neighbor's wedding and a mathematical description of the trajectories of the fundamental particles involved in the events of the wedding are descriptions of the very same activity, namely, the wedding. The physical events subsumed under the basic physical laws are thus better seen as the *ultimate material constituents* of the activities, achievements, and accomplishments whose forms physics has no business rehearsing.

Given this, Davidson's expression of the potential causal completeness of a scientific model of reality might be modified as follows. Every event will admit of a description of its *ultimate material constituents* in a vocabulary that allows those constituents to be brought under the aegis of natural laws. If that is so, there is still a clear sense in which our world is closed under purely natural causation; that is, the causal potential of each type of event is always and everywhere a matter of the laws of nature. The distribution of the chances of all future events would be fixed by the physical past and the laws of nature.

---

13. See "Causal Relations" and "The Material Mind," in Davidson's *Essays on Action and Events* (Oxford University Press, 1980). He writes as if the laws were not probabilistic, but this is no great matter.

It does not follow that the Highest One is absent from such a world. Nor, in such a world, need the Highest One be relegated to the role of Deism's watchmaker who winds up the world system, only to leave it to run on indefinitely on its own terms. The system of natural law, and the nomological character of individual causal transactions, may themselves be a manifestation of the Highest One, the way in which he continually "does" things; it may be that in which his almighty power consists.

So the causal mechanisms that lead to life, conscious awareness, and choice can be perfectly natural, that is, in accord with the laws of nature, and they may indeed take the form of random mutation and natural selection. As we shall see, this is compatible with certain objective constraints on what will be more or less viable, constraints that come not just from the physical structure of the environment but from the structure of reason or Logos. There may be concrete advantages involved in being a rational and loving being, and these advantages may be part of the *explanation* of the emergence of rational and loving beings at the end of an enormously long process of random variation and natural selection. Our interest in explanation is not merely an interest in the citation of basic causes, in the sense of the distributions of the fundamental constituents of things. Most of our explanations make no reference to that level of reality. We can make sense of a certain structure of reasons being a constraint without dabbling in the shallow and murky waters of "intelligent design"—that is, without adding a supercause to the already sufficient physical causes.

The Argument for Naturalism from True Religion

Once the distinction is made between naturalism as a methodological principle to the effect that we should always look to find naturalistic causes of events, and naturalism as an ontological thesis to the effect that the world is closed under purely natural causation, so that the causal potential of each type of event is always and everywhere a matter of the laws of nature, it is fitting to ask why we should accept the *ontological* thesis.

Ontological naturalists typically appeal to the "success" of science, guided as it has been by the methodological principle. But that argument can look like the product of survivorship bias. Many attempts at naturalistic explanations of phenomena have failed or have turned out to be refuted by later scientific discoveries. A host of failed naturalistic explanations languish in the dustbin of the history of science. We apply the honorific "science" to the manifestly successful applications of methodological naturalism. There has been a lot of success, and there has been a lot of failure. What are we to make of that?

I don't know. There is a delicate question as to how far the recognition of survivorship bias disables the argument from methodological naturalism to ontological naturalism.

There is, however, a religious argument not so much for ontological naturalism but for the proposition that we should hope that ontological naturalism is true. For ontological naturalism would be a complete defense against the supernatural powers and principalities that could otherwise exploit our tendency to servile idolatry and spiritual materialism.

One of the worst things that could happen to humanity appears in a recurrent popular fantasy. (It was predicted in advance by Carl Gustav Jung that this fantasy would emerge as a common fixation.) Here is one version of the fantasy. In the first act of the fantasy, representatives of a technologically advanced and apparently benevolent race of aliens land in front of the United Nations building in Manhattan; they sternly warn us about our bad characters, and offer to extend our lives indefinitely and make us gloriously happy, if only we accept and fall in with their larger plan for humanity, if only we declare fealty to their will.

The dark prediction is that most of us would accept the deal. Thanks to both the history of human selection and the nature of our partly self-molded characters, we are idolatrous, and we would not find it too degrading to live in servitude to another's will, as long as the other is sufficiently powerful and beneficent toward us. We want to be children again, not so much in the sense of having the simplicity of vision that Christ calls for when he insists that only the childlike can really find him, but in the sense of being relieved of the responsibility of living our lives out of our own fragile conception of the good. We would fear the aliens' power and would lust for the advantages they might confer us. Many of us would dedicate ourselves to placating the aliens, thereby enjoying the advantages that they confer on us, for we have already come to think that the way to live is to try to secure more and more advantage.

In the second act of the fantasy, the true intent of the aliens is revealed. It is, of course, anything but benign. They want to devour us, or use us for jet fuel, or whatever.

But we don't need the second act, which serves only to displace a deep anxiety onto something more concrete and imaginable. The aliens had already devoured us in the first act of the fantasy, and this would remain so even if they were truly benign, and remained benign, in their intent. For even then, they would have worked to cement us, or many of us, into lives organized around fear of power and lust for advantage.

The aliens of our fantasy are material beings, but the moral import of the fantasy would not change at all if they were imagined to be spiritual beings.

What human beings need is to be insulated against *any such deal*; and the advantage of ontological naturalism is that it would so insulate us, at least from the supernatural sources of such deals. (We shall, I am afraid, have to take our chances with the aliens, if any there be.)

Chapter 4

The Phenomenological Approach

THE METHOD AND THE QUESTION

Let us return from these all too brief remarks about naturalism versus scientism to our method and our question. The method was to take the foundational experiences of the major monotheisms on their own terms, and then look at the implied character of the spiritual beings who ostensibly appear in these experiences. The question was: Does the internal phenomenology of the foundational experiences of this or that version of monotheism display the character of the Highest One?

The method and the question cannot be dismissed merely as a tendentious piece of scientism directed at religion by the spiritually tone-deaf (the by-now-standard official "religious" response to the "undergraduate" atheists). For counterparts of the method and the question are integral to the monotheistic religions themselves. In each of the three religions, the question arises as to whether *this* (this behavior, this vision, this purported prophecy) comes from God, from man, or from an intermediate spiritual agency, such as a demon.

For example, there is in the Catholic, Orthodox, and Protestant traditions the idea known as "discernment of spirits." This is not what the *Wine Spectator* goes in for in its periodic subsections on the cognacs, the slivovitz, and the grappa; it is the attempt to assay the spiritual source and significance of an experience or manifestation by its content and aftereffects. The discernment of spirits is a general duty of the spiritual director, most notably during extended retreats, such as the Spiritual Exercises of St. Ignatius, in which the exercitant is susceptible to strong interior impressions, and even to visions. The spiritual director attempts to determine the source and significance of such interior impressions on the basis of the effects on the moral character and the aspirations of the exercitant. That overwhelming Light which inhabits the visual field of some exercitants around the third week of the Exercises, and which is sensed as a joyful revelation of the sheer intelligibility of things—could that be Lucifer himself? (Compare 2 Corinthians 11:14: "Satan transforms himself into an angel of light.") Well, the way to tell is to look at what the Light asks of the exercitant, and at what it prompts him to do.

Until recently, in the Catholic Church, a very particular form of the duty of discernment of spirits fell to the so-called Devil's Advocate, who was required to prepare the arguments against the canonization, the raising to the status of a saint, of any individual proposed for such an elevation. In the exercise of both the general and the particular duty, the phenomenology of the relevant religious experiences is taken at face value. The question then arises as to the character of the source and object of the experiences, a character partly determined by its effects.

The same issue of discernment of spirits or spiritual sources is found in the assessment of a prophet, or a messiah, or a gospel, as false. Recall 1 John 4:1:

> Beloved, believe not every spirit, but prove the spirits, whether they are of God; because many false prophets are gone out into the world.

Here, *internal* to religious orthodoxy is the deployment of a criterion of religious falsehood, a criterion that can be, in principle, brought to bear on the religious orthodoxy itself. Our method and our question can be seen as the attempt to raise the issue of discernment of spirits *in its full generality,* so that it becomes the issue of discernment of gods, that is, objects of worship.

YAHWEH'S USE OF THE METHOD

The issue of discernment of gods is broached, and answered in a magnificent way, in Psalm 82, a psalm that describes a Götterdämmerung. Yahweh there employs his own criterion of godliness, one by which the lesser gods (*elohim*) are found to be failures as gods. Consequently, he demotes them to the status of mere mortals.

The mythic scene setting of this psalm takes it as understood that Yahweh has given the lesser gods, the gods of "the peoples" or the gentiles, oversight and responsibility for those nations. (Compare Psalm 52 and Deuteronomy 32:8–9.) Yahweh then calls a heavenly assembly, rebukes these gods because of their indifference to justice, and strips them of their divine status.

> God presides in the divine council; in the midst of the gods he holds judgment;
> "How long will you judge unjustly and show partiality to the wicked?"

He reiterates his previous commands to them, thereby setting out what he requires of a god:

> Give justice to the weak and the orphan; maintain the right of the lowly and the destitute. Rescue the weak and the needy; deliver them from the hands of the wicked.

But in this the gods have failed, and have brought darkness and chaos to the earth:

> They have neither knowledge nor understanding,
> they walk around in darkness;
> all the foundations of the earth are shaken.

Yahweh then delivers his sentence:

> You are gods, children of the Most High, all of you;
> Nevertheless, you shall die like mortals, and fall like any prince.

In his commentary on this psalm, John Dominic Crossan writes:

> Psalm 82 tells us how we are to be judged by God but also how God wants to be judged by us. Everything else that God says or does in the Bible or life should be judged by that job description.

Is this or that the transcendental justice defined in Psalm 82 at
work? Or is this or that just transcendental testosterone?[1]

A CRITERION, OR AN ENCLOSED CIRCLE?

The eighty-second psalm sets out a criterion of godliness, a criterion
that in its turn applies to the Highest One. But to accept it as a correct
criterion, do we not have to take the psalm as expressing the view of
the Highest One himself? If so, it is an enclosed circle, into which
we cannot break, unless we have some antecedent conception of the
Highest One.

Yet the psalm does seem to produce a flash of recognition to the
effect that those lesser "gods" could not really be gods, and that anything likewise indifferent to justice could not be the Highest One. This
negative knowledge need not come from the purported revelation that
is the psalm itself. It could be the deliverance of some antecedent religious sense of things. Without such a sense, we could not hear the
psalm *as* expressing the character of the Highest One; we could at most
simply believe that it does on the testimony of the psalm itself, or on
the testimony of other parts of the Bible, about which the same question
of circularity could be raised.

There is a difference between hearing a purported revelation *as* expressing the character of the Highest One, and simply believing that it
does on the testimony of the ostensible revelation itself. This is shown
by the fact that whereas it is natural to hear Psalm 82 as expressing the
character of the Highest One, we cannot so easily do that with many
other psalms, as, for example, the so-called cursing psalms such as
Psalm 137:

O Babylon, you destroyer, happy those who return the evil you
have done us!

---

1. *The Birth of Christianity* (Harper Collins, 1998), 576–77. In invoking this passage. Crossan
may have known that the translation of *elohim* as it occurs in this passage as "god" is a matter of
some dispute. In an early study (1960) of Psalm 82, J. A. Emerton argued that in the early Aramaic
translations of the Hebrew Bible and in the renderings of the Psalms found in Qumran, *elohim*

Happy the man who shall seize and smash your little ones
against the rock!

As a matter of sheer phenomenology, it is just harder to hear this
prayer as properly directed to anything that would deserve the name of
the Highest One.

If that is right, and if there is a natural, if underdeveloped, religious
sense at work in these recognitions and absences of recognition, it need
only be that the religious sense delivers negative hints as to the criteria
of godliness. Nothing indifferent to justice, nothing open to hearing a
plea for the vengeful slaughter of innocents, could turn out to be the
Highest One.

But that may be enough to impugn the objects of worship in the
major monotheisms.

YAHWEH'S CRITERION APPLIED TO HIMSELF

How, then, does Yahweh himself fare by what John Dominic Crossan
calls God's own "job description"? Is he a just god, giving to each what
they are owed?

In asking this question, we court two dangers: one is to import our
modern conception of justice as fairness into another moral world in
which "justice" essentially meant covenantal or contractual justice between Yahweh and Israel. The other danger is to forget that the "job
description" of Psalm 82, the description with respect to which the
gods of the nations are found wanting as gods, itself goes far beyond
contractual justice, even to the point of requiring compassion for the
needy and the lowly.

In fact, the early Yahweh is himself truer to his own self-description
as "a jealous god, visiting the iniquity of the fathers upon the children
to the third and the fourth generation of those who hate me," than to

---

referred to angels. J. A. Emerton, "Some New Testament Notes," *Journal of Theological Studies* 2
(1960): 329–32. Even so, the moral point stands, or rather it holds a fortiori; if this is a requirement on the *angels*, how much more so must it hold of the Highest One. I thank Jan Cover for
raising the textual issue about the angels, and for the reference to Emerton's discussion.

the requirements of justice, fairness, and compassion. Yahweh is, as Exodus 3:15 puts it, "a man of war" ("der rechte Kriegsmann," in Martin Luther's ominous translation).

After all, Yahweh destroys the entire population of the earth by flood, except for the family of Noah. Many things can be said about this, but the first is that it looks on its face to be indiscriminate genocide. In Yahweh's defense, the Genesis text says that in those days the intent of every thought was evil, and continually so; but surely infants and the very young were not yet guilty in this way. And the wanton destruction of animal life was an integral part of this transcendental tantrum:

> Every living substance was destroyed which was on the face of the earth, both man and cattle and creeping things, and the fowl of the air. (Genesis 7:23)

Yahweh continues in the same genocidal spirit, hurling down burning sulfur on Sodom and Gomorrah (Genesis 19:24), and striking down all the firstborn of Egypt (Exodus 12:29). He urges Moses to impale those leaders of Israel who allowed the worship of Baal of Peor (Numbers 25). He demands that the Israelites take vengeance on the Midianites. When the Israelite army follows his orders, and kills every Midianite man, Yahweh is not satisfied, and he excoriates Israel for sparing the women and the children (Numbers 31)!

Yahweh's thoroughness in inciting and supporting mass killing is consistent, and extraordinary. It is by murder, and not by treaties or mercy, that Israel is directed to extend the land under its control.

> When the Lord your God brings you into the land you are entering to possess and drives out before you many nations . . . you must destroy them totally. Make no treaties with them, show them no mercy . . . do not look on them with pity . . . You must certainly put to the sword all who live in that town. Destroy it completely, both its people and its livestock. (Deuteronomy 7:1–16, and 13:15)

In fact, utter destruction, not only of the stigmatized human beings but *of their livestock*, is part of Yahweh's characteristic modus operandi.

In Joshua 6, for example, the Israelites under God's direction brutally destroy every man and woman, young and old, found in the city of Jericho; and not even the oxen are spared.

As Joshua and his armies continue the conquest of Canaan, they come upon the unfortunate inhabitants of the town of Ai; the ensuing description could have been the source of the chilling phrase "the killing fields":

> When Israel had finished killing all the men of Ai in the fields where they had chased them, and when every one of them had been put to the sword, all the Israelites returned to Ai and killed those who were in it. Twelve thousand men and women fell that day—all the people of Ai. (Joshua 8:24–26)

It would be incredible if among the twelve thousand hapless inhabitants of Ai, not to mention all of humanity before the Flood, none were weak or orphaned or lowly or destitute. Why, then, were they not protected by the justice laid down as Yahweh's own criterion of godliness in Psalm 82?

As for the people of Libnah, Makkedah, Gezer, Eglon, Hebron, Gaza, and Askelon, Judges 1:18 tells us that Joshua "left none remaining, but utterly destroyed all that breathed, as the Lord of Israel commanded."

Yahweh's anger is also famously kindled, and rekindled, against the Israelites themselves. Because they have ignored his prophets, Yahweh lets the Babylonians, led by Nebuchadnezzar, slaughter Israelite men and women—once again, young and old.

> They mocked God's messengers, despised his words and scoffed at his prophets until the wrath of the Lord was aroused against his people and there was no remedy. He brought against them the King of the Babylonians, who killed their young men with the sword in the sanctuary, and spared neither young man nor young woman, old man nor old woman. God handed them all over to Nebuchadnezzar. (2 Chronicles 36:16–17)

Chronicles mercifully spares us an account of the disposition of the Israelite livestock.

One could wade further into the sea of blood allegedly spilled with divine collusion, and dwell on the fate of the Moabites, the Perrizites, the people located in the stretch from Dan to Beersheba, and so on and so forth. But, frankly, it is a tale too sickening to recount in full.

Not only does the Bible explicitly credit Yahweh with the evils that befall Israel and its enemies; it also shows him in a suspicious relationship with *hassatan* (translated as "the Satan"), the adversary whom Yahweh sends to tempt men into evil, evil that Yahweh then punishes! In the book of Job, the Satan, a member of the heavenly assembly, is sent by God to tempt Job, a truly righteous man, to turn against God. Job perseveres in his faith through the most terrible suffering, and God wins his wager against the Satan.

So, also, the twenty-first chapter of the first book of Chronicles has it that the Satan was allowed to tempt David into the apparently blasphemous act of counting his people in a census. But when the second book of Samuel looks back on this same event, it says,

> And the anger of the Lord was kindled against Israel, and he [the Lord] incited David . . . to count the people. (2 Samuel 24:1)

The agency of the Satan here appears to be confounded with that of Yahweh!

The Satan, from time to time, mediates Yahweh's dark side. But it must also be noted that Yahweh is quite open about his own unmediated destructive capacities. Like an insecure patriarch, he constantly reminds his people through his prophets that he is a very dangerous person to mess with, that he is a source of great evil, as well as good. It is a central theme of the prophetic literature of the Bible. That will be denied, but only by those who have skipped over, or forgotten, the rather demented reiteration of the theme.

> I form the light and create darkness, I bring prosperity and create disaster; I, Yahweh, do all these things. (Isaiah 45:7)

Jeremiah is a particularly rich source of this kind of point.

> "Behold, I am bringing a nation against you from afar, O house of Israel" declares the Lord. "It is an enduring nation, it is an

ancient nation, a nation whose language you do not know, nor can you understand what they say. Their quivers are like open graves, their men are mighty. They will devour your harvest and your food; they will devour your sons and your daughters; they will devour your flocks and your herds." (Jeremiah 5:15–17)

Therefore, thus says Yahweh, Behold, I am bringing evil upon them which they cannot escape; though they cry to me, I will not listen to them. (Jeremiah 11:11)

And the people to whom they are prophesying will be cast into out-places of Jerusalem, because of famine, and the sword. They will have none burying them, not their wives, nor their sons, nor their daughters. And I have poured this out upon them because of their evil. (Jeremiah 14:16)

You shall say, 'Hear the word of Yahweh, O kings of Judah and inhabitants of Jerusalem. Thus says Yahweh of hosts, the Lord of Israel: Behold, I am bringing such evil upon this place that the ears of every one who hears of it will tingle.' (Jeremiah 19:3)

Thus says Yahweh: Behold, I am bringing upon this city and upon all its towns all the evil that I have pronounced against it, because they have stiffened their neck, refusing to hear my words. (Jeremiah 19:15)

Therefore their way shall be to them like slippery paths in the darkness, into which they shall be driven and fall; for I will bring evil upon them in the year of their punishment, says Yahweh. (Jeremiah 23:12)

Therefore, thus says Yahweh: Behold, I am bringing on Judah and all the inhabitants of Jerusalem all the evil that I have pronounced against them; because I have spoken to them and they have not listened, I have called to them and they have not answered. (Jeremiah 35:17)

The captain of the guard took Jeremiah aside and said to him,
Yahweh pronounced this evil against this place. (Jeremiah 40:2)

All the men who set their faces to go to Egypt to live there shall
die by the sword, by famine, and by pestilence; they shall have no
remnant or survivor from the evil which I will bring upon them.
(Jeremiah 42:17)

Thus says Yahweh: You have seen all the evil that I brought upon
Jerusalem and upon all the cities of Judah. Behold, this day they
are a desolation, and no one dwells in them. (Jeremiah 44:2)

For this day is the day of the Lord, Yahweh of Armies, a day of
vengeance, that he may avenge himself on his adversaries: and his
sword shall devour and be satiated, it shall drink its fill of their
blood. (Jeremiah 46:10)

I will terrify Elam before their enemies, and before those who seek
their life; I will bring evil upon them, in my fierce anger, says
Yahweh. I will send the sword after them, until I have consumed
them. (Jeremiah 49:37)

Is it not from the mouth of the Most High that good and evil
come? (Lamentations 3:38)

The other prophets present the same view of Yahweh as an agent of
destructive evil.

A third part of thee shall die with the pestilence, and with famine
shall they be consumed in the midst of thee: and a third part shall
fall by the sword round about thee; and I will scatter a third part
into all the winds, and I will draw out a sword after them. Thus
shall mine anger be accomplished, and I will cause my fury to rest
upon them, and I will be comforted: and they shall know that I
the Lord have spoken it in my zeal, when I have accomplished my
fury in them. (Ezekiel 5:13–14)

Therefore I will be unto them as a lion: as a leopard by the way will I observe them: I will meet them as a bear that is bereaved of her whelps, and will rend the caul of their heart, and there will I devour them like a lion. (Hosea 13:7–8)

Does evil befall a city, unless Yahweh has done it? (Amos 3:6)

Therefore thus says Yahweh: Behold, against this family I am devising evil, from which you cannot remove your necks; and you shall not walk haughtily, for it will be an evil time. (Micah 2:3)

Enough, you will say, is enough. Could it be that we have simply been too literalist in our blank presentation of these texts, forgetting that the Hebrew Bible is, among other things, a series of biographies of Yahweh in his dealings with Israel, biographies written by a variety of authors in a variety of historical contexts, all with their own embedded motives, both spiritual and political, so that we should expect jarring dissonance, rather than be surprised or shocked by it? And is not Yahweh being depicted by these various authors as *by and large* on the side of righteousness, at least as the authors conceived of it? This is a proper corrective, well applied to the likes of Dawkins's remark that Yahweh is "the most unpleasant character in all fiction."

That said, the theme of Yahweh's violence is a deliberate and persistent biblical trope, one that interpenetrates the great theme of his devotion to Israel. Try to play it down and you will underestimate the dramatic character of Yahweh's transformation, his second life as the advocate of justice and compassion.

On any but an esoteric interpretation of the many passages that are like those cited above, the Hebrew prophets appear to be speaking on behalf of a mercurial Patriarch, who can be bounteous and devoted to his favorites, but who is also obsessed with questions of respect, allegiance, and vengeance. At best, this appears to be an idolatrous projection onto the Highest One of the insecurities associated with the patriarchal psychological structure of ancient Near Eastern tribal life.

A sterner hypothesis was first offered by the second-century CE theologian Marcion and is taken for granted by modern reductive Historicists, namely, that in the religion of Yahweh, the Highest One never actually came into view. On the Historicist version of this hypothesis, the religion of Yahweh, which emerged in the late Bronze Age, was by historical accident simply the most successful of the contemporaneous cults, which included the cults of Zeus, Baal, Hadad, and Marduk. The success of the religion of Yahweh derived in part from the way in which it galvanized the Israelites against their enemies and reinforced their political self-assertion by means of an abiding sense of divine mandate.

By contrast, according to Marcion, Yahweh is indeed a god, and he is as depicted in the Hebrew Bible; but he is certainly not the Highest One, and he is not so much a god to be reckoned with as one to be passed by on the true path of spiritual development. For Marcion, he is at most the Creator of this world, not its Redeemer.[2]

In saying that, Marcion was expressing contempt for the religion of Yahweh, and so he is now described as having had contempt for Judaism. That is an anachronism on our part. It is precisely the spiritual achievement of the rabbis to have made Judaism something very much finer than the original cult of Yahweh. Marcion, writing in the second century CE, could have known little of this achievement.

In many ways, Rabbinic Judaism, by playing down the theme of Divine violence, and amplifying the theme of justice and love, is a religion that has tried to answer our second, collateral question on its own terms.

FORGIVING THE GOD

Human beings render the old gods irrelevant by coming to be better than they are; they shame the old gods by being better to the gods than the gods have been to them. These are the moments when a new spiritual dispensation is emerging, even if the human beings in question are not explicitly aware of this. Here is Jeremiah speaking, in Lamentations 3:

---

2. For a defense of something that harmonizes with Marcion's distinction between the god of creation and the god of salvation, see Peter Forrest's *Developmental Theism: From Pure Will to Unbounded Love* (Oxford University Press, 2007).

I am the man who has seen affliction by the rod of His wrath. He has led me and made me walk in darkness and not in light. Surely He has turned His hand against me time and time again throughout the day. He has aged my flesh and my skin, and broken my bones. He has besieged me and surrounded me with bitterness and woe. He has set me in dark places like the dead of long ago. He has hedged me in so that I cannot get out; He has made my chain heavy. Even when I cry and shout, He shuts out my prayer. He has blocked my ways with hewn stone; He has made my paths crooked. He has been to me a bear lying in wait, like a lion in ambush. He has turned aside my ways and torn me in pieces; He has made me desolate. He has bent His bow and set me up as a target for the arrow. He has caused the arrows of His quiver to pierce my loins. I have become the ridicule of all my people— their taunting song all the day. He has filled me with bitterness, He has made me drink wormwood. He has also broken my teeth with gravel, and covered me with ashes. He has moved my soul far from peace; I have forgotten prosperity. And I said, "My strength and my hope have perished from the Lord." Remember my affliction and roaming, the wormwood and the gall. My soul still remembers and sinks within me.

Instead of making the obvious inference from behavior to character, Jeremiah perseveres in his love for the Lord; he reminds himself of the Lord's better qualities, so as to continue to hope and trust.

This I recall to my mind, therefore I have hope. Through the Lord's mercies we are not consumed, because His compassions fail not. They are new every morning; great is Your faithfulness. "The Lord is my portion," says my soul, "Therefore I hope in Him!" The Lord is good to those who wait for Him, to the soul who seeks Him. It is good that one should hope and wait quietly for the salvation of the Lord. It is good for a man to bear the yoke in his youth. Let him sit alone and keep silent, because God has laid it on him; Let him put his mouth in the dust—there may yet be hope. Let him give his cheek to the one who strikes him, and

be full of reproach. For the Lord will not cast off forever. Though
He causes grief, yet He will show compassion according to the
multitude of His mercies. For He does not afflict willingly, nor
grieve the children of men.[3]

It is a heartbreaking confession of faithfulness in the face of overwhelming reason to give up. Children of abusive parents would rather
inhabit a hell in which those parents are still present, than a heaven in
which they are absent. Just as such a child deserves better parents, Jeremiah deserves a better god.

A Reply to Yahweh's Answer to Job

If, prior to revelation, we can know that the Highest One is not indifferent to justice, and is not a perpetrator of evil, then we must conclude
either that Yahweh (in his first life) is not the Highest One, or that he
is so encrusted with the anxious projections of ancient Near Eastern
patriarchy that his true nature as the Highest One is obscured by the
very tradition that is directed toward him.

But, it will be said, *who are we* to so flatter ourselves as to suppose
that we could have knowledge, even negative knowledge, of the nature
of the Highest One prior to his revelation of himself? Recall Yahweh's
answer to Job's protest at the injustice of the terrible suffering visited
upon him by Yahweh and his collaborator, the Satan.

Then the Lord answered Job out of the whirlwind, and said "Who
is this that darkens counsel by words without knowledge? Gird
up now thy loins like a man; for I demand that you answer me.
Where were you when I laid the foundations of the earth?" (Job
39:1–4)

And again:

---

3. Again, I thank Jan Cover for reminding me of this passage. He, however, places a quite
different construction on it.

"Will you also annul my judgment? Will you condemn me, that you may be righteous? Have you an arm like God? Can you thunder with a voice like him? Deck thyself out with majesty and excellence; and array thyself with glory and beauty." (Job 40:8–9)

It is an assertion of Yahweh's immense power, and, by implication, of his supreme moral authority. What would *we* know of the Highest One, prior to his own revelation of himself? Where were *we*, when he made the Leviathan, or set the foundations of the earth? Who are we to judge *him*?

(What exactly is the intended inference from great power to supreme moral authority, a moral authority that would silence any antecedent sense of injustice?)

Presumably the same answer, the invocation of the power and majesty of the Highest One, would be given to those who agonize over what Yahweh asks of Abraham by way of a demonstration of fealty, namely, that he intend to sacrifice his only son, Isaac. *Who are we* to set limits in advance on what the Highest One could require? Could not the Highest One "suspend the ethical" as Søren Kierkegaard put it, and ask anything, just anything, of Abraham?[4]

Well, suppose Abraham had been ordered to *eat* his son, or do something worse to him. Could the Highest One *really* teach us that cannibalism or child molestation could be contemplated as fitting tributes to his will? We do know the answer to that. A being who proposed such things, and tried to get us to intend them, as a test of our commitment to him, would not be the Highest One. Can anyone seriously claim otherwise?

The unfortunate fact is that such claims have been made; but in making them, their proponents have fallen into a certain kind of incoherence. If we do indeed lack even such a minimal grip on what the Highest One could or could not ask of us, then the very possibility of his revealing himself to us begins to unravel. That is the consequence of a line of thought which distinguishes a truly religious experience that is ostensibly *of* the Highest One from an impressive experience

---

4. See Søren Kierkegaard, *Fear and Trembling* (Everyman's Library, 1994).

of extraordinary events which leads on to *a conclusion* about the
Highest One.

A revelation of the Highest One could not just consist in an experience whose whole content was that of an impressive event, such as a
loud basso voice booming from the heavens, the sun's whirling around
the sky, or a dry path opening across the Red Sea. There is nothing
particularly religious about such strange events; and the experience of
them as such does not deserve the name of religious experience, even
if a theological construction is *subsequently* placed on the experience.
The experience of the strange, the tremendous, or the mysterious, plus
a theological construction placed on that experience, still falls short of
an experience in which the Highest One seems to be revealed.

What more is required? The human being who is the beneficiary of
a revelation must see or hear the events *as* the Highest One manifesting
himself. That content must be internal to the experience and not just
to the subsequent beliefs that it prompts.

Now the philosophers tell us that a condition of seeing or hearing
something as *so and so* is that one have some antecedent concept, be it
occurrent or dispositional, of the so and so in question. The philosophers say, for example, that you can't see a table *as a snooker table*
unless you have some idea of what a snooker table is. So if the original
recipients of revelation had any business extending their fealty as a result of their experiences, then they must have heard or seen the revelatory events *as* revelations of the Highest One. And they could not have
done this without some antecedent concept of what would and would
not count as the Highest One.

This is, if you like, a sketch of an argument from a standard philosophical account of seeing or hearing something *as such and so*, and
the phenomenology of the foundational revelations of the major
monotheisms, to the existence of an antecedent, if only partial and
dispositional, conception of the Highest One. Without it, the ostensibly
foundational experiences of the major monotheisms could not have
taken place. All the originators could have actually experienced, *in the
sense of actually enjoyed as the content of their experience*, would have
been impressive events: extraordinary sights and sounds that could
equally well have been experienced as expressions of lower spiritual
forces. At the level of belief, the originators might have placed this or

that further construal on those experiences, as, say, effects of the High-est One, but the experiences *themselves* would not be experiences of the Highest One.

But, so the religions of revelation tell us, this is not in fact the way in which Abraham or Moses heard or saw the events by which Yahweh revealed himself to them. The content of those religious experiences, what would have to hold if those experiences were veridical, did not leave open the possibility that something other than the Highest One was manifesting itself. Abraham and Moses heard the sounds and saw the sights *as* the Highest One addressing them. So they must have had an antecedent, if only partial, conception of the Highest One, one not wholly provided to them by the revelations in question.

By this consideration it can be seen that those who wish to obliterate the legitimacy of any antecedent religious sense of things, in order to underline the radical nature of the revelation of the Highest One, are confused. The logic of seeing and hearing *as* makes some antecedent religious sense of things a *precondition* of the revelation of the Highest One. Yes, God is transcendent, and so known *de re* to us only by his revelation; but for that revelation to occur, there must be antecedent *de dicto* knowledge of something of the nature of the Highest One.

It remains to be seen what such an antecedent religious sense or conception might come to, how it might be refined, and what it might entail.

Chapter 5

Is There an Internal Criterion
of Religious Falsehood?

In the execrated Regensburg lecture, Pope Benedict deploys a criterion of religious falsehood, indeed a criterion of godliness, against the very idea that the Highest One could order his people to use violence as a means to either convert or overcome unbelievers. Unfortunately, the pope's radical criterion was wholly masked by the public reaction. Benedict's lecture seemed to his critics to be just an intricate way of opening up a familiar line of criticism of Islam as a religion that tolerates, and even encourages, violence.

Against that simple interpretation of what the pope was up to, it must be remembered that at the time of his election to the papacy, Benedict had just spent twenty-five years of his life as prefect of the Congregation for the Doctrine of the Faith. So he can only have been vividly aware of the actual methods used by the Congregation in the bloody days of yore when it was known under its antique and ominous title "The Office of the Roman and Universal Inquisition."

Further, the Holy Father is more than familiar with the fact that the Hebrew Bible is littered with examples of Yahweh ordering his people to violence. Perhaps this is why, utterly amazingly, he writes of "the often toilsome and tortuous threads of biblical faith." The pope needs no tutelage to the effect that each of the three monotheisms has much to answer for when it comes to religious violence, and indeed that each has fallen into a deadly form of piety by helping itself to the conviction that *Deus volt.* (He cannot, for example, have forgotten the millions who died as a result of the Crusaders' repeated and hapless attempts to conquer the Holy Land.) The same worry about "openness to violence" could be raised for each of the three monotheisms, and Benedict knows this as well as anyone does.

The truly remarkable thing about the Regensburg lecture has been overlooked in the intense media controversy caused by the pope's quotation of Emperor Manuel II's remark: "Show me just what Muhammad brought that was new, and there you will find things only evil and inhuman, such as his command to spread by the sword the faith he preached." (The pope's text emphasizes that he finds in these words "a startling brusqueness, a brusqueness that we find unacceptable." Actually, that does seem a slightly odd way of putting it. Is it only the brusqueness that is unacceptable? Would a more *suave* formulation of the same charge be acceptable?)

The pope's extraordinary lecture must be quoted at some length, because only then can we see how radical a theologian we are actually dealing with in the person of Benedict, one who is prepared to put a test to claims of Divinity.

Benedict writes of an "inner rapprochement between Biblical faith and Greek philosophical inquiry." This, he says,

> was an event of decisive importance not only from the standpoint of the history of religions, but also from that of world history.

Benedict sees a first stirring of that "inner rapprochement" *even in Yahweh's revelation of his true name to Moses!*

> In point of fact, this rapprochement had been going on for some time. The mysterious name of God, revealed from the burning bush, a name which separates this God from all other divinities with their many names and simply asserts being, "I am", already presents a challenge to the notion of myth, to which Socrates' attempt to vanquish and transcend myth stands in close analogy. Within the Old Testament, the process which started at the burning bush came to new maturity at the time of the Exile, when the God of Israel, an Israel now deprived of its land and worship, was proclaimed as the God of heaven and earth and described in a simple formula which echoes the words uttered at the burning bush: "I am". This new understanding of God is accompanied by a kind of enlightenment, which finds stark expression in the mockery of gods who are merely the work of human hands (cf. Psalm 115). Thus, despite the bitter conflict with those Hellenistic

rulers who sought to accommodate it forcibly to the customs and idolatrous cult of the Greeks, biblical faith, in the Hellenistic period, encountered the best of Greek thought at a deep level, resulting in a mutual enrichment evident especially in the later wisdom literature.

Benedict is sensitive to the charge that his theological emphasis on reason is merely an ethnocentric attachment to one local and specific cultural form. This he correctly and decisively rejects.

As far as the understanding of God, and thus the concrete practice of religion, is concerned, we are faced with an unavoidable dilemma. Is the conviction that acting unreasonably contradicts God's nature merely a Greek idea, or is it always and intrinsically true?

The answer is that it is always and intrinsically true.

I believe that here we can see the profound harmony between what is Greek in the best sense of the word and the biblical understanding of faith in God. Modifying the first verse of the Book of Genesis, the first verse of the whole Bible, John began the prologue of his Gospel with the words: "In the beginning was the λόγος". This is the very word used by the emperor [The Byzantine emperor Manuel II]: God acts, σὺν λόγω, with *logos*. *Logos* means both reason and word—a reason which is creative and capable of self-communication, precisely as reason. John thus spoke the final word on the biblical concept of God, and in this word all the often toilsome and tortuous threads of biblical faith find their culmination and synthesis.

Benedict, here sounding more and more like his philosopher-countryman Jürgen Habermas,[1] interprets *Logos* as publicly accessible

---

1. See their friendly dialogue *The Dialectics of Secularization: On Reason and Religion* (Ignatius Press, 2006).

reason understood as an objective constraint on all actual reasoning and communication.

Benedict is of the conviction that the insertion of the Greek theme of Logos into biblical faith was ordained, rather than merely adventitious:

> The encounter between the Biblical message and Greek thought did not happen by chance. The vision of Saint Paul, who saw the roads to Asia barred and in a dream saw a Macedonian man plead with him: "Come over to Macedonia and help us!" (cf. *Acts* 16:6–10)—this vision can be interpreted as a "distillation" of the intrinsic necessity of a rapprochement between Biblical faith and Greek inquiry.[2]

Moreover, in Benedict's view, the Septuagint's Hellenized translation and partial transmogrification of the Old Testament is *a new step in the ongoing revelation of God's nature!*

> Today we know that the Greek translation of the Old Testament produced at Alexandria—the Septuagint—is more than a simple (and in that sense really less than satisfactory) translation of the Hebrew text: it is an independent textual witness and a distinct and important step in the history of revelation, one which brought about this encounter in a way that was decisive for the birth and spread of Christianity. A profound encounter of faith and reason is taking place here, an encounter between genuine enlightenment and religion. From the very heart of Christian faith and, at the same time, the heart of Greek thought now joined to faith, Manuel II was able to say: Not to act "with *logos*" is contrary to God's nature.

It is this severance of God and reason that Benedict finds so worrying in what he takes to be Islam:

---

2. The pope might also have mentioned Paul's remarkable sermon on Mars Hill as to the true identity of the Athenians' unknown god.

The decisive statement in [Manual II's] argument against violent conversion is this: not to act in accordance with reason is contrary to God's nature. The editor, Theodore Khoury, observes: For the emperor, as a Byzantine shaped by Greek philosophy, this statement is self-evident. But for Muslim teaching, God is absolutely transcendent. His will is not bound up with any of our categories, even that of rationality. . . . Ibn Hazm went so far as to state that God is not bound even by his own word, and that nothing would oblige him to reveal the truth to us. Were it God's will, we would even have to practice idolatry.

Benedict then discerns a disturbing theological connection linking Islam, Protestantism, and Kant. Just as the aforementioned version of Islam fails to appreciate the full revelation of God as Logos, the attempt during the Reformation by Luther, Calvin, and Zwingli to purge Christianity of its Platonic and Aristotelian legacy was nothing less than a misunderstanding of the full Christian revelation of God as Logos:

Dehellenization first emerges in connection with the postulates of the Reformation in the sixteenth century. Looking at the tradition of scholastic theology, the Reformers thought they were confronted with a faith system totally conditioned by philosophy, that is to say an articulation of the faith based on an alien system of thought. As a result, faith no longer appeared as a living historical Word but as one element of an overarching philosophical system. The principle of *sola scriptura*, on the other hand, sought faith in its pure, primordial form, as originally found in the biblical Word. Metaphysics appeared as a premise derived from another source, from which faith had to be liberated in order to become once more fully itself. When Kant stated that he needed to set thinking aside in order to make room for faith, he carried this program forward with a radicalism that the Reformers could never have foreseen. He thus anchored faith exclusively in practical reason, denying it access to reality as a whole.

Even Paul's epistles, notable for their overt hostility to Greek intellectualism, and their alternative emphasis on agapeistic love as the manifestation of the Divine, are represented by Benedict as consistent with his theme:

> Certainly, love, as Saint Paul says, "transcends" knowledge and is thereby capable of perceiving more than thought alone (cf. Ephesians 3:19); nonetheless it continues to be love of the God who is *Logos*. Consequently, Christian worship is, again to quote Paul—"λογικὴ λατρεία", worship in harmony with the eternal Word and with our reason (cf. Romans 12:1)

These are extraordinary propositions, which taken together go far beyond the traditional Catholic legacy of the mere *harmony* of revelation and natural reason. For Benedict is saying that the deliverances of reason are an ineliminable part of the full revelation itself. Indeed, the deliverances of reason have a kind of veto power over other purported Judeo-Christian revelations, the *"often toilsome and tortuous threads of biblical faith."* The pope said that? The text of the Regensburg lecture remains on the Vatican's website at the time of this writing.[3]

A Consequence of the Pope's Criterion

The Regensburg lecture thus presents a religion of Logos or reason. Reason, properly understood, has a veto on claims of other parts of revelation. God cannot do anything contrary to reason. If God cannot do anything contrary to reason, then either the gods of the three monotheisms are not God, or they are God, but seen only through a very, very dark glass.

The initial obscurity in the content of Benedict's criterion of religious falsehood lies in the systematic ambiguity of "reason" as a translation of *Logos*. We should distinguish the purely formal reason of mathematical logic and decision theory from the substantive, even sweet, reasonableness that abjures violence and makes real communication possible.

---

3. www.vatican.va/holy_father/benedict_xvi/speeches/2006/september.

From the point of view of purely formal reason, one man's substantive irrationality can be another man's revelation. For why is it not rational to suppose, as the Inquisitors did, that one is doing a favor to the heretic to torture him into compliance with orthodoxy; after all, his immortal soul is at risk. Compared to its salvation, what are a few days of torture deployed to loosen the heretical soul's attachment to its selfish will?

In this reasoning there is no mistake in mathematical logic, and no failure to apply the canons of decision theory.

Still, it is perverse.

One answer as to why it is perverse, and it seems to be Benedict's answer, is that to require torture for salvation could not lie in the nature of the Highest One. So we could not be carrying out his will in torturing the heretic or the schismatic.

Surely that is right, and surely it is something we know by the light of natural reason. A god who told us otherwise would not be the Highest One. (But once again, that is a proposition whose form is negative; it specifies only something about what the Highest One is not.)

The truly remarkable element in Benedict's lecture is that these naturally knowable propositions, propositions known to Plato, Aristotle, and the Stoics, form part of the full Christian revelation, rather than merely providing an extraneous criterion for religious falsity. Of course, it is none of our business to follow the pope in that.

Religious and Scientific Fallibilism

No believer can claim to be free of resistance to the Highest One, especially the form of resistance that misrepresents idolatrous compensations as ways of turning one's life into an expression of fealty to his will. But we might be able to begin to imagine and describe what a *less* idolatrous conception would look like.

Before turning to that, let us stay for a moment with the idea of a criterion of religious falsehood. The availability of such a criterion makes room for the pleasing possibility of religious fallibilism, according to which the three monotheisms are each incomplete, and partly occluding, visions of the Highest One. That, of course, would have the implication that they might work together to arrive at a less occluding vision of this same One, a project that makes sense only if there is an agreed-upon criterion of religious falsity. It would also require abandoning the irenic maneuvers encountered earlier, such as the "friendly" attempts to assimilate another's "God." Such maneuvers simply mask the critical questions that an honest religious fallibilism, and an honest ecumenism, must work through. (As if science could have progressed by ecumenically treating special relativity and Newton's theory as essentially the same thing.)

Therein lies the practical interest of the rhetoric of idolatrousness common to the major monotheisms. *It contains at least the germ of a common criterion of religious falsity.* We should neither underestimate the difficulty of developing that common criterion in an effective way, nor overdo the contrast with the idea of a criterion of falsity common to the practitioners of a given field of science.

Fallibilism is the doctrine that a theory or outlook, however well credentialed, is likely to contain falsehood. That is the natural philosophical view to take of those scientific theories that aspire to general descriptions of the universe on the basis of what must of necessity be very limited and local observations. Scientific generalization is not a matter of deduction from observations; it relies crucially on induction, or inference to the apparently best explanation of the observed phenomena.

Formed as they are in this way, the generalities that constitute our favored scientific theory are underdetermined by the available evidence. A host of other theories, most of them unknown to us, could also accommodate the restricted range of phenomena we have observed. Hence the open-ended and self-critical orientation of the best science, in which the practice is not to defend the best theory we have so far, but to look for new observations that will falsify our presently best theory and so force that theory to undergo evolution toward (what we hope is) a better approximation to the truth.

As an attitude, fallibilism can be kept alive in science because there is an agreed-upon criterion of the falsity of scientific theories, namely, their implying something ultimately at odds with observation. Yet, and here is the first step in any serious thought about scientific method, as Pierre Duhem famously pointed out, being ultimately at odds with observation is no simple matter.[4] A scientific theory might be said to entail that our observations will be thus and so, but it does this only in conjunction with auxiliary hypotheses that bridge the gaps between theory, experimental design, and human observation. So there is room for judgment as to when we have a genuine counterexample, and when we have a "confounding variable," a name for something going wrong that should not be blamed on the theory under test.

Moreover, as Carl Hempel showed us, the fallibilist attitude itself complicates the idea that observation can refute a theory.[5] If one is a fallibilist, one will recognize that one's present set of generalizations do not constitute a complete theory of reality, or even a complete theory of the domain of one's particular science. One will expect that there could well be certain unknown mechanisms of nature that would make for anomalous observations, observations that are not properly taken to discredit the limited scientific theory that one presently has.

This realization leads to a cautious tendency to treat one's generalizations as "ceteris paribus" generalizations—that is, as generalizations not in the style of "All ravens are black," but in the style of "Other things being equal, all ravens are black." The latter, qualified or "ceteris paribus," generalization expresses the recognition that there may well be as-yet-unknown mechanisms that now and then make for the odd albino raven. The point of the qualified generalization is to set those cases aside as irrelevant to the theory at hand.

Having seen this so clearly, Hempel asked a characteristically good question: Why doesn't this sort of endemic qualification make science vacuous; for "ceteris paribus" is such an opened-ended notion that one might allow under the rubric of irrelevant cases all the counterexamples that come up, so that "ceteris paribus" in "Ceteris paribus, all ravens are black" amounts to the weasel clause "so long as we are not dealing with the irrelevant case of a nonblack raven"?

Hempel's appealing answer was that part of the training in any given science, and in its characteristic art of generalization, is acquiring

---

4. *The Aim and Structure of Physical Theory*, trans. Philip P. Wiener (Princeton University Press, 1954).

5. C. Hempel, "Provisos," in *The Limits of Deductivism*, ed. A. Grunbaum and W. Salmon (University of California Press, 1988).

knowledge, often largely tacit knowledge, of what would count as an irrelevant confounding variable, as against a genuine counterexample. It is this acquired knowledge that allows a scientist to rely on ceteris paribus generalizations in a way that does not make scientific generalization perfectly vacuous.

If you are to function as a scientist, it is not enough to learn the latest theories. You have to learn what a real counterexample would look like in your particular field of science, and this has something of the character of being initiated into a way of seeing how your subject matter hangs together. It falls outside the purview of any formal theory of induction or probabilistic reasoning. It is, you might say, a matter of discernment. Without this common acquired discernment, there would not be the level of intersubjective agreement on the meaning of experimental outcomes that makes science viable as a collective practice. Here, as elsewhere, substantive reasonableness, and not mere compliance with the canons of formal rationality, is a necessary condition for any collective deepening of understanding. And we have to be trained into traditions of substantive reasonableness.

But now suppose that Benedict is right, and the Highest One cannot do anything at odds with substantive reasonableness. Where, then, can we find the religious traditions of substantive reasonableness that could shed some light on the nature and purpose of the Highest One? As it turns out, they are spread across Judaism, Christianity, and Islam, and concentrated in the thoughts of a Persian physician, a Spanish rabbi, and an Italian monk, particularly in their reflections on the *via analogia*.

As we shall see, within these thoughts there is something that leads to a view of the Highest One that is at odds with ontological monotheism, and closer to what is known as "panentheism."

Chapter 6

Why God?

Doesn't Substantive Reasonableness Suffice?

So there is a kind of acquired discernment, indispensable in science and everyday life (and Benedict suggests that it is also indispensable in religious belief), a discernment that allows one to appreciate the force of considerations that go beyond those of pure logic, and beyond the deliverances of decision theory as applied to our standing beliefs and desires. Among these considerations or *substantive reasons* are not only theoretical reasons but practical reasons, reasons that bear on what we should desire and do. Now many philosophers suppose that at the very least, the ethical—what is valuable or worthy as an object of desire or pursuit—and what properly informed substantive reasonableness would ultimately favor, must be coextensive.[1]

Here we are retreading the well-worn pathways of so-called ethical monotheism, and thinking of God as *Logos* gradually disclosing the requirements of substantive reasonableness, and so of the ethical. An obvious question arises: Why do we need God at all? Why do we need to think of our developing sense of substantive reasonableness as the gradual disclosure of an already complete and fully adequate conception, a *Logos* already present in the Divine Mind?

Can't the ethical stand on its own? Why need it be backed by the threats and promises of a Divine Judge? (Or, as J. S. Mill less sympathetically put it, by "moral bribery and the subornation of the understanding?")[2] Doesn't the force of reason itself demand to be respected, *how-*

---

1. For different but related views of the connection between what is valuable and what substantive reasonableness upholds, see John Rawls's "Outline of a Decision Procedure in Ethics," *Philosophical Review* 60 (1951), and the Aristotelian Society Symposium on "Dispositional Theories of Value" consisting of David Lewis, Michael Smith, and myself. See *Proceedings of the Aristotelian Society,* supplementary vol. (1989).

2. John Stuart Mill, "The Utility of Religion," in *Three Essays on Religion* (Hackett, 1998), 119.

ever we understand its origins? Can we not, then, see "God" as an idea that has gradually lost its usefulness, as a consequence of the hard-won historical development of our richer, though still incomplete, understanding of substantive reasonableness and its requirements? (This is the familiar narrative of secularism as a supersession, a necessary purging of religiosity from the ethical.)[3] Indeed, even if we recognize the large-scale defects of human life as something to which we need to be reconciled, isn't a this-worldly philosophy enough to preserve faith in the importance of goodness?[4]

The believer's response will be that even if we were to allow this, there nonetheless remains the fact that God has revealed, or is revealing, not only the ethical path for human beings as such, but his more specific plans for us: for example; as his covenant-bound Chosen People, or as his sons and daughters in Christ, or as his true servants in the *Dar al-Tawhid*.

It should now go without saying that our phenomenological method, which brackets the question of existence, cannot adjudicate whether any of these more particular claims are true. Is there, then, anything else that can be said, simply out of an antecedent religious sense of things, one not tied to any specific putative revelation, anything that would point to any need for further talk of God? I believe there is, and I believe that when properly articulated, it is something we can hardly deny, even if the idea was given its first decisive formulation within the Judeo-Christian tradition.

We are, in a certain way, fallen creatures; our wills are utterly compromised by self-will, and, left to our own devices, we at best live out adventitious and conventional conceptions of the good, conceptions that are in many ways parodies of the ethical, properly understood. The only thing that can set us right is a *katalepsis*, a seizure by grace, something transformative entering from outside our fallen natures.

If that is granted, perhaps in the light of the considerations adduced below, then the first question of monotheism, the question of whether

---

3. For a brilliant anatomization of this theme of supersession, and an extended treatment of its inadequacies, see Charles Taylor's *A Secular Age* (Harvard University Press, 2008).

4. A question taken up in my *Surviving Death*.

there is one God, must be rephrased in an urgent *practical* form. Do the various forms of grace—the various ways in which human beings are captured by something that at the same time overcomes the centripetal force of the self and turns them toward the ethical—have a *common* source? Are they all, indeed, manifestations of the Highest One?

They could be, but only if the Highest One is more than the monotheisms have allowed. That is the burden of what follows.

The Fall

Now the serpent was more cunning than any beast of the field which the Lord God had made. The serpent said to the woman, "Did God actually say, 'You shall not eat of any tree in the garden'?" And the woman said to the serpent, "We may eat of the fruit of the trees in the garden, but God said, 'You shall not eat of the fruit of the tree that is in the midst of the garden, neither shall you touch it, lest you die.'" But the serpent said to the woman, "You will surely not die. For God knows that when you eat of it your eyes will be opened, and you will be like God, knowing good and evil." So when the woman saw that the tree was good for food, and that it was a delight to the eyes, and that the tree was to be desired to make one wise, she took of its fruit and ate, and she also gave some to her husband who was with her, and he ate. Then the eyes of both were opened, and they knew that they were naked. And they sewed fig leaves together and made themselves loincloths. (Genesis 3:1–7)

The idea of the Fall, the idea of original sin, is minimally the idea that there is something deeply problematic that comes with the condition of being human. Yet in falling, Eve exhibits just two faults, a certain self-will, manifested in her disobedience, and a longing for wisdom—knowledge of good and evil—*from the tree*. Why does that combination entail her, and our, expulsion from Paradise?

What moralists sometimes call "self-love" or "self-will," the tendency to seek premium treatment for oneself at significant cost to others, has its roots in the very structure of consciousness. One's own consciousness, the arena of presence and action in which and out of which each one of us lives our lives, presents itself as a fundamental context for the worldly happenings that make up the details of one's life. So long as we are alive, we ourselves are always around; every time we wake up in a chair or in bed, there we are, coeval with the appearance and reappearance of the world. And so we operate as if the world just wouldn't be the world unless we were HERE, as it were, at the center of it. In this way it can seem as if we are the fountainhead of the very reality we inhabit.

To probe a little more into this: each one of us *finds* him- or herself at the center of an arena of presence and action. This arena can be thought of as a composite psychological field, consisting of one's perceptual field, the field of bodily sensation, and the field of imagination and thought. The modes of presentation of the items in one's perceptual field are perspectival; that is, they present items to a particular viewing position, or more generally to a particular point from which someone might sense the surrounding environment. The implied position at which those modes of presentation seem to converge is the position of one's head and body. To that same implied position, a bodily field, as it were a three-dimensional volume of bodily sensation, also presents. And that implied position is also one from which certain acts, presented as willed, emanate. Furthermore, it is the position where mental acts seem to be available for higher-order awareness. And when mental "images" and sounds are generated by imagination in a space detached from their respective fields—as when one imagines the Hindenburg bursting into flames or rehearses a tune "in one's head"— those imagined items appear at the center.

Let us call this whole centered pattern, existing at a particular time, and perhaps over time, as it were the apparent mental *bed* in which one's "stream of consciousness" flows, *an arena of presence and action*. There is one such arena HERE, and each person can make a corresponding remark that holds true in his or her own case.

All that is to say that there is given in my experience an "intentional object" that appears to bound my thought and experience, and makes it seem like a unified whole. And this bound or arena is structured around another intentional object, the implied position to which external items and mental events present. Again, I assume it is like this in

your own case as well. Each one of us finds him- or herself at the center
of an arena of presence and action.

To use my own case as an illustration of the general case: it is the
property of being at the center of THIS arena of presence that is *the
property of being me* in the most intimate and important sense. It is
because the human being Johnston is at the center of this arena of presence that he *is* me. I wake up, in bed or in a chair, and there is Johnston
occupying the central phenomenological position. If it had turned out
that it was someone else here at the center of this arena of presence, say
Mother Teresa, or John Locke's Rational Parrot, or the Prince of Darkness, then I would have been that woman, or that parrot, or that fallen
angel. My self-love would then have extended to the woman, or to the
parrot, or to the angel. For a person's being HERE, AT THE CENTER OF
THIS, seems to justify extending self-love to him. What else could?

The basic form of individual human life is not so much Being There,
but Being Here, at the virtual center.[5]

Each arena defines a "HERE" and a "THERE" in a fundamental
way. Each one of us discovers himself or herself at the relevant "HERE,"
and the rest of the world correspondingly "THERE." But this is not a
mere theoretical distinction; the arena does not just present two apparent "places" that seem to be on a par. Those places are surrounded
by a massive asymmetry of affect that presents what is HERE as, in effect,
especially valuable, to be prized and protected, while it presents what
is THERE as a set of opportunities and obstacles, potential benefits and
threats for the prized thing found HERE. Of course, the affective
asymmetry is dispositional; it does not have to be raging all the time.
But in times of stress or threat or anxiety the asymmetry is palpable,
and it provides a default starting point for subsequent emotion,
thought, and action.[6]

---

5. These remarks are in part taken from *Surviving Death*, where the arena, and the illusion of
separate selfhood it helps create, are explored in detail.

J. J. Valberg, following Zeno Vendler and Thomas Nagel, offers the most detailed and insightful
account of the centered nature of the phenomenology of self-consciousness to be found in the
analytic tradition. See his wonderful book, *Dream, Death, and the Self* (Princeton University Press,
2007). The comparisons and contrasts between Valberg's "horizon" and the arena are treated in
an addendum to chap. 2 of *Surviving Death*.

6. On affect as ostensible disclosure of value see my "The Authority of Affect," *Philosophy and
Phenomenological Research* 61 (2001).

Here we have a basic orientation that structures the consciousness of the higher animals. Perhaps the arena is an effective way to organize animal consciousness, to make for an operative preverbal distinction between SELF and NOT-SELF, and to mobilize the animal's energies around protecting the animal that is SELF.

Let us now consider the question of the Fall. What happens when that peculiar thing, the *human* animal, makes its appearance on earth? What happens when an extended capacity for self-consciousness, an extensive symbolic memory, and an impressive capacity for practical deliberation to action are added to this basic orientation of animal consciousness? How do these enhanced capacities interact with the experienced arena, and with the basic evaluative asymmetry between "HERE" and "THERE"?

One thing that emerges is a developed sense of one's own life as extending out of a remembered past into an anticipated future, a future that is sensed as capable of being shaped by one's practical deliberation toward action. This brings with it a sense of one's life as something *to be lived*; that is, shaped according to some conception of the worthy or the good—some conception that would provide at various times in one's life more or less consistent reasons to continue to live one's life in a certain way, and so allow for meaningful deliberative effort in life, rather than just living by whim.

Such conceptions of the worthy or the good can initially be absorbed only from those around us. They are validated by our community to the extent that those conceptions dovetail with our community's interests, indeed with the interests of the various communities we inhabit. The conceptions must then be, or appear to be, partly *other-regarding* conceptions of what is worthy or good; that is, they must be conceptions that represent some putative ways of benefiting others as themselves good, worthy, even demanded.

Some sense of the prima facie legitimacy of other-regarding demands—some kind of conscience—is thus a widespread feature of the human form of self-consciousness. This has two notable causes. One is our felt demand to give some direction to our lives, to shape our lives to some degree by some conception (it might in fact be confused or perverted) of what is worthy, a conception that we can consult at various moments of deliberation to action, whatever variation in our whims and fancies might occur across those moments. The second is our initial lack of originality when it comes to such conceptions; we have no choice but to absorb them from the others, and what they have on offer will invariably be conceptions of the good that are to some extent other-regarding. So we all come into a detailed world of evaluation, a world in which what is to be done, how one is to live, and what is to be avoided appear to be more or less settled in advance. We are thrown into some context or other in which we find our wills already bound, at least de jure, if not de facto, by preestablished other-regarding conceptions of what is good or worthy.

Psychologically opposed to this, each one's extended self-consciousness makes explicit the fact that he or she is at the center of an arena of presence. Constantly finding oneself at the center, one finds oneself to be privileged—as something to be protected, as something to be prized. Thanks to our extended self-consciousness and our capacity to articulate what we find, what was in the higher animals merely an organizing form of animal self-protectiveness now becomes something more. It becomes a more or less explicit deliberative theme, a default starting point in one's practical reasoning: one's own interests just seem paramount. Hence self-will, the tendency to put one's finger on one's own side of the scales, a tendency whose real motto is "I am to be given premium treatment."

The psychological urgency of self-interest sits uneasily with the other-regarding conceptions of the good that one has absorbed. Neither is stably experienced as a wholly appropriate object of the will; and so there is the familiar cycle of self-will, obedience to "the Law," guilt at failure, effort at improvement, and the inevitable lapse into self-indulgence. One is a secret, or not so secret, betrayer of the very good one has internalized.

At the same time "the Law"—the conception of the good one has internalized from the others—is likely to be compromised in fundamental ways. First, it is likely to be "averaged out." In order to be commonly available from the others and for all, it must prescind from the detailed lineaments of this or that temperament, personality, or character; in the worst case it is a pair of pants meant to fit all, which in fact produces close to universal discomfort. (Or it evades this problem by enormous flexibility, by turning a blind eye to near universal defection in a variety of circumstances, so that those who passed the conception of the good on to us seem either impossibly lax or hypocritical.)

Second, the conception of the good on offer from the others is likely to have the unquestionable character of an embedded natural conviction, something that *they know* to be the right way of going on, a knowledge that each defends by pointing to what is commonly taken as obvious. So it can present itself in the guise of an unquestionable necessity.

And third, a conventionally available conception of the good needs to be collectively defended. For it functions as an answer that can silence the question "How am I then to live?"—a question that would be terrible if left unanswered, because then we would have no practical way of responding to the demand that we *live our life*. Without some such conception, we are left to face the terror that there may be no way to live our life, nothing worth doing between now and the moment of our death. Because adhering to the conception reduces the threat of this terror, the conception will be defended with a certain violent intensity, an intensity that comes not from the reasoned sense that there is after all something to be said for it, but from repressed anxiety: without *this* way to live our lives there may be *no* way to live our lives. This terror of conscience, the felt but unanswered need to live one's life out of some conception of the good, is a kind of *existential* threat; it threatens the very possibility of our existing as deliberative, and hence as human, beings.

Here we have the natural source of the idolatrous element in "works righteousness" or respectability; an adventitious and compromised conception of the way to live is rigidly held to, and treated as an absolute, because of an inability to face the terror that might come from challenging it.

One sign of this repressed existential anxiety lies in the violence associated with the policing of the common conception of the good; the stigmatizing of those who have found other ways to live; and the cathartic scapegoating of the transgressors. (About which, more later, in the discussion of René Girard's theme of the cathartic function of symbolic sacrifice.)

This means that the common conception of the good, even though it may in fact be a conception of intrinsic goods, things that are indeed worthy of pursuit in themselves, can actually function as mostly instrumental, in that it mainly serves to block a terrible, and still unresolved, anxiety about how to live. So part of our fallen condition consists in the fact that what we rely on to silence the call of conscience, the question of how to live our life, is an internalized adventitious conception of the good that is compromised in at least three ways: in its averageness, in its appearing as a false necessity, and in its functioning as a defense mechanism against existential anxiety.

Original sin, the sin that comes with the condition of being human, is thus not just the self-will that resists the other-regarding demands built into one's internalized conception of the good. It is self-will combined with a covetous and violent protection of the compromised fruit we have plucked from the tree of knowledge of good and evil.

Here, then, is an interpretation of the myth of the Fall. Paradise is not for us because we are by our natures caught in an oscillation between self-will and false righteousness. Neither is a happy resting place.

Homo Incurvatus in Se

Our nature, by the corruption of the first sin being so deeply curved in on itself (*incurvatus in se*) that it not only bends the best gifts of God towards itself and enjoys them, as is plain in the works-righteous and the hypocrites, or rather even uses God himself in order to attain these gifts, but it also fails to realize that it so wickedly, curvedly, and viciously seeks all things, even God, for its own sake. (Martin Luther, *Lectures on Romans*, L515–L516)

We arrive at uneasy compromises, pushed as we are by the forces of self-love and the less than satisfactory common conventional understanding of the good, the worthy, the sacred, or the heroic. One such compromise is "works righteousness," that is, a condition of respectability in which one does, and is known to do, the conventionally right thing. The best that can be said for respectability or works righteousness is that those who police the boundaries of the conventionalized good, including our own internalized versions of such figures, can then be expected to leave us alone.

The respectable life is not itself an ethical life, nor is the ethical life merely an intensification of the respectable life. You can become more respectable without approaching the ethical life any more closely. The ethical life does not consist in the triumph over self-will by way of moral effort directed at the conventionalized good. That triumph is not so much a way of breaking out of the cycle of self-will, obedience to "The Law," guilt at failure, effort at improvement, and the inevitable lapse into self-indulgence, as a way of locking oneself into one stage in the cycle, obedience to "the Law." And there is considerable evidence that the triumph of moral effort over self-will—for example, in what is called "the authoritarian personality"—is far from costless when it comes to the virtues of flexibility, openness, self-directed irony, and an appreciation of the festive character of life. (Think of Luther the monk, and his grim and idolatrous religiosity, as he himself confesses it.) That is one sign that the rigorously respectable life is not the ethical life.

What of the no doubt attractive, and even to some degree excellent, life of a person who has the ordinary virtues of self-confidence, flexibility, openness, self-directed irony, perseverance, fair-dealing, moderation, and good judgment? Is this not the ethical life? All would have been well with this, it seems, had it not been for the apparently authoritative announcement that the Reign of God is at hand, and the associated commands, expressed for example in Mark 12:30–31:

> Thou shalt love the Lord thy God with all thy heart, and with all thy soul, and with all thy mind, and with all thy strength: this is the first commandment. And the second is like unto this: Thou shalt love thy neighbor as thyself.[7]

The claim of the life of ordinary virtue to be the ethical life is nullified by such an announcement and such commands, at least if they are truly authoritative.

Absent the authority to repeat the announcement or the commands, for this would be to outright endorse a revelation peculiar to one of

---

7. Compare Leviticus 19:18: "You shall not take vengeance, nor bear any grudge against the sons of your people, but you shall love your neighbor as yourself; I am the LORD."

the monotheisms, we are still left with two things that speak against the claims of the life of ordinary virtue to be the ethical life.

One is the reminder that the apparent self-sustainability of the ordinary virtuous life is merely apparent, given the large-scale structural defects of human life. Those defects present themselves either as destructive fates that will obliterate much of the significance of virtue, or as intimations that there is something more than ordinary virtue.

The second thing, and this testifies to great dignity of philosophy, is the description here and there within the philosophical tradition of a form of life distinct from and arguably higher than the virtuous life. Thus philosophy keeps to the old promise of *ex veritate vita*.

The truly ethical life is a life in which you encounter yourself as one person among others, all equally real. This means that the legitimate interests of others, insofar as you can anticipate them, will figure on a par with your own legitimate interests in your practical reasoning— that is, in your reasoning as to what you should do and what you should prefer to happen. Inevitably, given that each one of the others counts the same as you in your practical reasoning, the interests of others often will swamp your interests in your own practical reasoning as to what you should do and prefer. For you will find yourself to be only one of the others, the one you happen to know so much about, thanks to being him or her. Here I follow Thomas Nagel in identifying the ethical life with a life whose guiding principle is radical altruism or *agape*.[8]

As many have pointed out, the ethical life in this sense is madly demanding, and one of the things that it puts in jeopardy is the very ability to live a meaningful life, in the ordinary sense of that term.[9] A meaningful life is a delicate cross-time construction, put together with some care by the agent whose life it is. It requires a systematic implementation of the agent's distinctive conception of what is valuable; and this in its turn involves a certain blindness to, and even ob-

---

8. See Thomas Nagel, *The Possibility of Altruism* (Princeton University Press, 1975).

9. See, for example, Susan Wolf, "Moral Saints," *Journal of Philosophy* 79 (1982), and R. M. Adams's reply, "Saints," *Journal of Philosophy* 81, no. 7 (1984).

tuseness about, the radical needs, and hence the legitimate interests, of all those others.[10]

We already find in Kant something like the following thought: the only sustainable meaning available in an ethical life is the ethical itself; that is the distinctive value of finding yourself as just one among others equally real, the value of having a good will—as Kant put it, "the only thing in this world or in any other which is valuable in itself." But this, the philosophical rearticulation of the highest ethical ideal found in Judaism and Christianity, in Hillel and in Christ, is simply madness when ripped out of the religious frame in which it first appeared.[11]

Kant himself would have been among the last to deny the condition that Augustine and Luther describe as "Homo incurvatus in se," the condition of man being turned in upon himself.[12] Kant has a vivid sense of the overwhelming centripetal force of illegitimate self-love. Famously, he asserts that we are radically evil. By this Kant does not mean that we are bad to the bone and, hence, irredeemably evil. He means that by nature each one of us demands premium treatment for himself; each sets his own interest up as an overriding principle of his will, so that each is really an enemy of the others and of the ethical itself.

It is, of course, a problem within the Kantian philosophy just how Kant could consistently allow that he knows such a universal and, it seems, necessary truth; for Kant takes those features to be the reliable sign of the a priori. And what are we to make of the idea that it is a priori that we are radically evil? Even so, we can endorse Kant's view a posteriori: the existence of the arena, the fundamental asymmetry of value that it presents, and the effects of adding to the arena the human capacity for extended self-consciousness and deliberation to action—

10. See Peter Ungar, *Living High and Letting Die: Our Illusion of Innocence* (Oxford University Press, 1996).

11. For a detailed defense of this, see John E. Hare, *The Moral Gap: Kantian Ethics, Human Limits, and God's Assistance* (Oxford University Press, 1998).

12. For a telling exploration of this theological theme of incurvature, from its roots in Augustine, through Luther and Karl Barth, see Matt Jenson, *The Gravity of Sin: Augustine, Luther and Barth on Homo incurvatus in se* (T & T Clark, 2007).

taken together, these predict that we *will* be radically or naturally evil in Kant's sense.

But what is the source of redemption from natural evil in Kant? Given that we are radically evil, then, if we have no source of redemption, do we not have a proof from Kantian premises that our sense of the demands of the moral ought are simply illusory. For ought implies can, and we can't, at least not left to our own devices. To be sure, Kant thought that there were proofs of the immortality of the soul, of the freedom of the will, and of a just God who will come to judge us, proofs from the preconditions of moral action and the rational hope that there should be a situation in which just desert and happiness are correlated. Still, the conclusions of these proofs are propositions that we would be required to believe if Kant's arguments are good. But belief in a proposition cannot redeem us from the condition of being *incurvatus in se*.

THE REDEEMER?

We are left with the anti-Kantian argument, the argument that Kant perhaps *should have given*: the moral ought, the felt demand that our wills should be good or be made good, and so be moved by the interests of all considered equally, is a complete illusion. For ought implies can, and because we are radically evil, we actually *can't* make our wills good.

The conclusion of that argument provokes moral despair, but we cannot back out of it by denying that we are radically evil, at least when this is properly understood. Could we try to become less evil, less turned in upon ourselves? Well, not simply by our own intentional act or acts. For those acts would have maxims, and those maxims would inevitably be rendered crooked by the centripetal force of self-love. Being radically evil, that is, natural opponents of the ethical life, we naturally can will only evil; that is, we can act only on maxims conditioned by our self-interest. So left to our own devices, willing our own improvement is just another cunning form the evil will can take. (Yes, we can become more respectable by our own effort, and by effort and training we can even become more virtuous in the ordinary sense. But these are not movements within the ethical life, at least as Kant presents it.)

Here Kant's moral theory presents as a philosophical appropriation of Christianity, an appropriation that is inconsistent because it is incomplete. We are in a condition of natural or original sin, but the ethical demand is something like the demand of *agape*, on its face an impossible demand given the centripetal force of self-love.

Kant has sin and *agape*, but no redeemer. Is it not the case that the existence of a redeemer, a source of grace—that is, something transformative entering from outside our fallen natures—is also in need of being deduced as another "postulate of practical reason," a belief required if we are to avoid moral despair?[13]

Kant's problem is our problem, at least if we allow that something like *agape* constitutes the ethical life, and admit that human beings are naturally turned in upon themselves in sin. We need a redeemer, an external source of grace that could overcome the centripetal force of self-will.

We now must face some questions that have been hovering over all of the foregoing. Are not the sources of redemptive *katalepsis*, or grace,

---

13. For Kant, what is supposed to overcome the centripetal force of self-will is the "feeling" of respect for the moral law. But the question is why such a feeling should be effective as a motive. Without an answer to that, "respect for the moral law" can sound simply like the proper outcome, though wrongly invoked as if it were an actual cause of that outcome.

That salvation from sin is an explicit, though not fully thematized, issue for Kant is suggested by passages like the following from the *Conflict of the Faculties*, Ak VII, 43:

> If by nature we mean the principle that impels us to promote our happiness, and by grace the incomprehensible moral disposition in us—that is, the principle of pure morality—then nature and grace not only differ from each other but often come into conflict. But if by nature (in the practical sense) we mean our ability to achieve certain ends by our own powers in general, then grace is none other than the nature of the human being insofar as he is determined to actions by a principle which is intrinsic to his own being, but supersensible (the thought of his duty). Since we want to explain this principle, although we know no further ground for it, we represent it as a stimulus to good produced in us by God, the predisposition to which we did not establish in ourselves, and so, as grace.—That is to say, sin (evil in human nature) has made penal law necessary (as if for slaves); grace, however, is the hope that good will develop in us—a hope awakened by belief in our original moral predisposition to good and by the example of humanity as pleasing to God in his son.

Thanks to Desmond Hogan for a very helpful discussion of this point.

many and various? So if we were to deduce the existence of redemptive grace, as another postulate of practical reason, another precondition of the avoidance of moral despair, would it not be more honest to locate the variety of the forms of grace within the framework of polytheism rather than that of monotheism? If the sources of grace are many, then what is to be made of the idea that we find our salvation in this most singular thing, the Highest One?

If it is to be of salvific interest, then the Highest One must be a unity that embraces this diversity, so that although the sources of grace are many, they in their turn have a common source. And perhaps their effects are intensified when they are seen as coming from this common source.

Chapter 7

After Monotheism

The Highest One

The inner truth of the ban on idolatry is best understood as the requirement that our worship be directed to the Highest One, and only to the Highest One. We do know that if there is a Highest One, there can be nothing that is more deserving of our fealty. We also know that if there is a Highest One, it deserves our fealty, not arbitrarily, but because of its perfections. We need not know what those perfections are; in fact our very idea of perfection may be extremely limited, but we do know that there can be none more perfect than the Highest One. Otherwise, that Other One would be the one to turn to for salvation.

Suppose that there is something created by the Highest One, but nonetheless *distinct* from the Highest One, in that it is not some part, aspect, principle, or mode of the Highest One. Call this other thing "the separate creation." If there is such a separate creation, then we would expect the perfections of the Highest One to be to some extent reflected in that separate creation. Consider, then, the joint reality made up of the Highest One and the separate creation. It would seem that this joint reality might be a more appropriate object of worship than the subpart of the reality that is the Highest One. Or, at the very least, the joint reality would be an appropriate object of fealty that was not identical with the Highest One. But this is inherently at odds with our principle that the Highest One and only the Highest One deserves worship. So there is no separate creation. What is called creation is some part or aspect or principle or mode of the Highest One. That is why a worshipful attitude to the whole of reality is not idolatrous. It is not worship of creatures as such; they are seen only as manifestations of the Highest One.

This, to be sure, is a much too compressed argument for the doctrine that the Highest One includes his creatures as manifestations, aspects, or modifications. Perhaps, for example, something about the supposed whole disqualifies this whole as an object of worship. (But what could it be? Well, it might be that reality as a whole has no will to which we can declare fealty. But if the Highest One has a will, then surely creatures will be an expression of that will, and so the whole can be said to manifest a will to which one can declare fealty.) Still, the argument can serve merely as an illustration of how knowledge of mostly negative propositions concerning the Highest One might condition our conception of his relation to the whole of reality.

Another example may help to make that point. About the Highest One something more can be said without the grace of revelation, and merely by dint of natural reason. His goodness cannot be augmented by that of any other being. The existence of other beings can further express, but not augment, the goodness of the Highest One. Otherwise the combination or sum or union of other beings and the supposed Highest One would be still Higher, that is, more worthy of worship, fealty, and love. It would be a better competitor for the name of the Highest One. Of course there can be no such competitor. But then those other beings, which have some good in them, can only be modes or manifestations of the Highest One. This is a step toward the idea that the Highest One includes all beings as his modes or manifestations; what would complete the journey is the old mysterious premise to the effect that all being is good.

The Tetragrammaton

Common to the three great monotheisms is the conviction that the Highest One revealed himself to Moses. Even in the midst of the burning bush, Moses was clearheaded enough to check the credentials of his interlocutor; and so we have the revelation of the tetragrammaton, the four-syllabled, nature-revealing name of God. The passage is worth quoting again.

> "But," said Moses to God, "when I go to the Israelites and say to them, 'The god of your fathers has sent me to you,' if they ask

me, 'What is his name?' what am I to tell them?" God replied, "I am who am." Then he added, "This is what you shall tell the Israelites: I AM sent me to you." (Exodus 3:13–14)

Taken as a revelation of the Highest One's nature, the tetragrammaton goes beyond anything that could be delivered by the antecedent religious sense. Indeed, even assimilating that revelation has proved difficult for monotheistic theology. Who or what is the Highest One saying he is?

Perhaps the best-known and most developed answer is given by Thomas Aquinas. On Thomas's view, in the disclosure of the tetragrammaton, the Highest One reveals himself as "Ipsum Esse," that is, Being, or Existence Itself. In the end, this turns out to be a profoundly Platonic construal of the revelation of the tetragrammaton.

Aquinas is clear that he does not mean by this that the Highest One is introducing himself as the universal property of being an existent, the rather empty property shared by all the things that exist. God is not a property. Instead, as emerges in Thomas's theory of analogical predication, Existence Itself is something like a Platonic *eidos*, of which the existence of Socrates and the existence of Fido, and the existence of each and every other thing are examples. Aquinas thinks of the existence of Socrates as the thing in virtue of which Socrates exists, and the existence of Fido as the thing in virtue of which Fido exists. All such things, all creaturely *existences*, are examples of Existence Itself. Each creature thus exists by participating in Existence Itself. But this does not augment Existence Itself so much as express it in detailed finite ways. As the Thomistic tag has it: after creation there are more beings, but not more Being. (There is no such thing as making more Being, any more than there is making more Red.)[1]

---

1. The idea of Existence Itself may seem to make no sense to those who suppose that all we need to express existence is the particular quantifier "some," so that existence is not a predicate, not a property, and certainly not an *eidos*. But the idea of the particular quantifier as expressing not just quantity but existence seems at odds with the logical coherence of certain thoughts, such as the thought that some things have been prevented from existing. That may be a false thought, but it is not logically incoherent. Consider a process that by its natural operation would lead to the coming into being of some definite thing; say a particular dog coming into being from some specific embryo. If that process is terminated at a certain point, then the particular dog that would have come into existence was prevented from coming into existence. So some dog was prevented

Whereas in the case of the creaturely examples of Existence, we can distinguish between the essence of the thing in question and the existence of the thing in question, and conceive of the essence's remaining unrealized so that the creature might not have existed, there is no such room to allow for the essence of Existence Itself apart from its existence.

Once the Platonistic frame of creaturely existents as tropes or examples of Existence Itself is placed around our experience of reality, there is then no doubting that Existence Itself—that is, God as Aquinas conceives him—is real. For we perceive that there are existents; and so the eminent exemplar, Existence Itself, exists. Given the Platonistic frame, every creature thus testifies to the existence of God. This is not so much an argument for the existence of God as a way of seeing reality so that the question of God's nonexistence cannot arise. And here, even in his abstruse philosophy, Aquinas radiates a vivid sense of *the fact of God*, with respect to which the "five ways" are (not wholly adequate) argumentative expressions.

All one can say by way of resistance to the Thomistic God is either that you can't see creatures as individual examples of Existence Itself or that there is something even Higher.

The content of this overtly Platonic construal of the Highest One's self-revelation to Moses could be captured in a different idiom—for example, in Paul Tillich's terms to the effect that the Highest One is the Ground of our Being, that is, the thing part of whose exemplification is our very existence. Putting it that way may help to discharge a false sense of Existence Itself as fabulously abstract rather than the most concrete aspect of things, the aspect in which we move and live and have our being. The exemplification of Existence Itself, something that can be analogized to a self-giving act, is just the whole of reality.

Compare this affirmation of both the transcendence and the immanence of the Highest One to the opening lines of the *Tao Te Ching*, which have the foundational principle pervading and sustaining all manifestation, and yet never in the slightest way being used up by this creative activity.

---

from coming into existence. So "some" is not existentially loaded as a matter of its context-independent meaning.

There is a thing inherent and natural
Which existed before heaven and earth
Motionless and fathomless it stands alone and never changes
It pervades everywhere and never becomes exhausted

. . .

I do not know its name, but I call it Tao
I name it Transcendent.

Now: there is a profound inner tension introduced into monotheism by these reflections on the tetragrammaton. If the Highest One has actually announced that he is Being or Existence Itself, then much of what counts as sacred writ and law is merely a projection of our anxieties and fixations onto the Highest One.

It is no good trying to dismiss that thought by repeating the old denigrating remarks about the god of faith versus the god of the philosophers; for, as Benedict himself emphasizes, the god of faith introduces himself in terms that invite characterization by way of Greek, and in particular Platonic, philosophical idiom.

If the Highest One is Existence Itself, then much of the description of the Highest One in the three monotheisms is at best metaphor, allegory, a series of honorific titles, or a web of analogy. Existence Itself cannot literally be "a jealous God, visiting the iniquity of the fathers upon the children to the third and the fourth generation."

That kind of consideration has itself led many to simply reject Existence Itself as "the god of the philosophers, not the god of faith." But that familiar gambit is busted once we think ourselves inside the ban on idolatry (a main point of the foregoing). For as we shall see, once Existence Itself truly comes into view, it is then much more difficult (though not impossible) to conceive of a Higher One. And after Existence Itself comes more clearly into view, it will seem patently idolatrous to regard the anthropomorphic accretions of this or that historical faith as definitive of the Highest One.

THE PARADOX OF THE HIGHEST ONE

Yet perhaps the very idea of the Highest One is somehow incoherent. This is, anyway, how it begins to look if we play out the traditional idea that the Highest One is the First One in the order of being, something "ontologically prior," as the philosophers say, to everything else. That philosophical gloss on the monotheistic tradition is actually very natural and seems encouraged by passages like this:

> Who has performed these deeds? He who has called forth the generations since the beginning. I, the Lord, am the first, and with the last I will also be. (Isaiah 41:4)

There is a medieval line of thought about the consequent *simplicity* of the Highest One, a line of thought that in the end is quite destructive of any coherent positive conception of God. (At best, it would leave us in the position of those noble ones who build a temple to "The Highest One, Whoever or Whatever That Is.") The line of thought, which should be put to rest once and for all, begins with a positive account of why the Highest One deserves our worship. It is not just that the Highest One deserves our worship because of his perfections. He deserves our worship because of his unique place in the structure of reality. The Highest One deserves our worship because he is the *absolute source* of reality. Which is to say that any reality, such as a separate creation, that is not identical to the Highest One must be ontologically dependent on the Highest One; that is, the full account of *what it is to be* this other reality must invoke the Highest One as the source or principle of this other reality.

None of the "living idols" and the lesser spiritual beings whose worship is proscribed by the ban on idolatry are the absolute source of the reality of those who worship them. That is an important part of why worship directed at the "living idols" and the lesser beings is misdirected. For it cannot be a way of confronting that which reveals one's deepest nature as a dependent or "created" being. This can be revealed only in a confrontation with the absolute source of reality.

As the absolute source of reality, the Highest One is not ontologically dependent on anything else. It cannot owe what it is to a combination of things, any of which it is not. For then it would not be the absolute source of reality.

The doctrine that the Highest One cannot be ontologically dependent on anything else has been taken to imply the following striking— I would say ultimately paradoxical—conclusion. The essence of the

Highest One, the thing that would be captured in an account of what it is to be the Highest One, is simple. That is, this essence is not in any way a composite or combination of properties, principles, parts, modes, or aspects. Otherwise the Highest One would not be the absolute source of reality. It would not be, as Aquinas puts it, "the First Being," the first in the order of being, the order of ontological dependence. So worship directed at it would be misdirected.

Aquinas gives the canonical form of the argument in *Summa Theologica* 1.3.7, immediately after offering his famous five proofs or "five ways" to the existence of God.

> Every composite thing is posterior to its components and dependent on them. But, as was shown above, God is the First Being.

So the absolute source of reality cannot be in any way complex. Aquinas goes further and argues that even the complexity that comes from the distinctness of the existence of a thing and what that thing is—its essence or essential attributes—cannot be found in the First Being:

> In every simple thing, its being and *that which it is* are the same. For if the one were not the other, simplicity would be removed. As we have shown, however, God is absolutely simple. Hence, in God, being good is not anything distinct from him; he *is* his Goodness. (*Summa Contra Gentiles* 1.38)

And the same would hold for his Justice, and for his Power, and for each of his other essential attributes. He *is* his Justice and his Goodness and his Power!

Augustine had already arrived at this very conclusion in *De Trinitate* 6.7.8:

> We speak of God in many ways—as great, good, wise, blessed, true, and whatever else does not seem unworthily said of him. Nonetheless, God is identical with his greatness, which is his wisdom (since he is not great by virtue of quantity, but by virtue of power); and he is identical with his goodness, which is his wisdom and his greatness; and he is identical with his truth, which is all of these things. For in him it is not one thing to be blessed and

another to be great, or wise, or true, or to be good, or to be alto-
gether himself.

This theological tradition tells us that because the absolute source of
reality must be *a se*—that is, from itself, and from no other—it is therefore not ontologically dependent on anything else for either its essence
or its existence. But if it were composite, then it would owe its essence,
and perhaps its existence, to the items of which it is composed. Therefore it is simple.

The step from "aseity" to simplicity is one thing, but why must the
Highest One, as the absolute source or the First Being, be such that all
its essential attributes are *identical*? Doesn't that depend, as Nicholas
Wolterstorff has suggested in a seminal article, on the optional philosophical view of a thing's essential attributes as components of that
thing?[2] And so here, as elsewhere, the tradition of natural theology
appears to be projecting an optional philosophical picture onto the
Highest One.

As against Wolterstorff's important suggestion, this paradoxical
transition from aseity to the conclusion that the First Being cannot
have properties in the way that other beings do, but must somehow
be its properties, can indeed draw support from the alternative philosophical picture of the relation between properties or attributes and
their bearers or subjects. On this alternative, something has an attribute
not by having that attribute as a component, but by instantiating the
attribute. Instantiation is here understood as an external relation to
an attribute, understood as distinct from what instantiates it. So, for
example, if the First Being is good, then it is good in virtue of instantiating the attribute Goodness.

But where do these distinct attributes come in the order of being?
They, too, must be ontologically dependent on the First Being, which
is to say that their essence is to be explained in terms of the essence of
the First Being and not vice versa. Now, so the tradition tells us, the
First Being is essentially good. And this cannot consist in a relation to
what is ontologically dependent on the First Being, namely, the attri-

2. "Divine Simplicity," *Philosophical Perspectives* 5 (1991).

bute of Goodness. For then we would have to appeal to something, namely, Goodness, that is ontologically dependent on the First Being, in order to explain the essence of the First Being. But the First Being's being First—that is, absolutely ontologically prior, the absolute source of reality—precludes this. For if something is to be absolutely ontologically prior, then the account of what it is to be that thing cannot invoke other *distinct* beings (such as attributes) that are ontologically dependent on that thing.

The conclusion is, then, that the First Being cannot have properties or attributes, either as plural components, or by instantiating them.

The remaining alternative appears to be the genuinely paradoxical one, explicitly endorsed by Augustine and Aquinas, namely, that the First Being *is* its attributes. Otherwise it could not be First; otherwise it could not be the absolute source of reality.

Why is this paradoxical? Because it entails what might be termed "the identity theory of God's nature," namely, that God himself is identical with his Goodness, and is identical with his Existence, and with his Justice and with whatever other attributes are truly predicated of him. This, in its turn, entails that God is a single property or attribute. Now we are no longer engaging with monotheism at all. The simplest philosophical elaboration of God as the First in the order of Being breaks all connection with the monotheistic faiths.[3]

Are the monotheisms, then, just directed at gods? Is it that there are only gods, since the notion of the Highest One refutes itself?

There have been various attempts to avoid this conclusion. Each consists in clarifying just what is involved in thinking or speaking of the Highest One.

SPEAKING OF THE HIGHEST ONE

One of the great forms of resistance to anthropomorphic projections onto the nature of the Highest One, and so one of the great forms of

---

3. I follow those interpreters of Plato who treat the *eide* as preeminent particulars, not properties or attributes. For a discussion of why monotheism makes little sense if God is a property or attribute, see Alvin Plantinga, *Does God Have a Nature?* (Marquette University Press, 1980).

resistance to idolatry, has been the Jewish, Christian, and Islamic tradition of dwelling on the meaning of the "Divine Names," the honorifics canonically applied to God within these traditions. The heroes of this tradition are Ibn Sina, Maimonides, and Aquinas. (And they should be required reading for the revivers of undergraduate atheism, who are happy to rattle off predications of the god they aim to show does not exist.)

The question central to this tradition expresses a self-critical theological insight: When we name or describe God through his supposed attributes, what could we reasonably be attempting to do? After all, anything that deserves to be known as the Highest One will be so unlike us that our very thoughts and concepts, which are tools for coping with the everyday reality of the world of creatures, will not be made for him. (We know already that the gendered pronoun "him" is wildly out of place, but there it is.) So in what sense can we take seriously our characterizations of him as just, or good, or powerful, or wise?

In the *Guide for the Perplexed* the great medieval rabbi Moses Maimonides (1135–1204) makes a three-way distinction among talk of what God is not, talk of God's actions in the world, and talk of God's inherent attributes.[4] Maimonides accepts the argument from *aseity* to divine simplicity; he accordingly regards all literal predication of inherent attributes directed at God as incoherent, for he supposes that such predications would imply complexity in the Divine Nature. So for Maimonides, the same argument that shows that God cannot be a body, because then he would have parts outside of parts, and so be complex, shows that God cannot have a plurality either of inherent essential attributes or of inherent accidents.

Maimonides then offers a reconstructive account of the apparent predication of the familiar attributes of God. When we say, repeating what has been revealed to us of God, that

God is just

one thing in the vicinity that we can mean, *and have come out true*, is an honorific predication of the form

4. *Guide for the Perplexed*, trans. Shlomo Pines (University of Chicago Press, 1963), 111–47.

God is the Just One

which is in effect an identification of God with himself, picked out by the honorific title "the Just One."

The various honorific predications

God is the Just One
God is the Wise One
God is the All-powerful One

are all made true by the same fact, a fact of identity, namely, that God is God. So no complexity in God's nature is implied by the variety of honorific predications that our tradition of worship encourages us to make.

According to Maimonides, when we say, "God is just," another thing in the vicinity that we can mean and have come out true is a purely negative proposition to the effect that

God is not unjust.

The litany of such negative propositions does not imply any complexity in God's nature. So there is no problem in principle with supposing that such negative propositions can be literally true even when taken all together.

Maimonides' account of our predication of attributes of God is thus a double reconstruction, not of what we meant, but of all we could reasonably have meant. For Maimonides, to think we could traffic in true literal predication of intrinsic attributes of God is in effect an expression of the idolatrous urge to contain God in an image or representation. Positive theology emerges as a kind of intellectualized idolatry.

However, when it comes to talk of God's extrinsic actions in the world, Maimonides offers a third account of the nearest thing we could mean and have come out true. The Bible is full of reference to God's actions, such as God's *vengeance* against the Israelites. Maimonides thinks that what makes this an appropriate way of talking is that there is an *analogy* between certain divinely instituted effects involving the Israelites, and human vengeance. When we say

> God took vengeance on Israel

we are speaking by analogy with human vengeance, and what makes what we say true is that there is a definite analogue of aspects of human vengeance in the divinely instituted effects (say, the destruction of the Temple in the wake of a betrayal of the covenant by the Israelites).

The doctrine of analogy is one of the richest ideas in medieval philosophy and theology. Aquinas is particularly famous for applying that doctrine to the very category of predications that Maimonides treated in such a revisionary mode, namely, predication of the honorific attributes of God. (In this, Aquinas followed and deepened the views of Ibn Sina (980–1037), the great Muslim physician and philosopher whose Neoplatonic interpretation of Aristotle helped shape Western Scholasticism.)[5]

Aquinas begins by making what is, for his philosophical contemporaries, already a familiar distinction between univocal, analogical, and equivocal predication. In employing the first kind of predication, we are saying the very same thing of any subject we use the predicate to characterize; and with the third kind of predication we can be saying an entirely different thing in different uses of the predicate, as when we predicate "pen" of a writing implement and then of an animal's

---

5. As a backhanded testimony to the longevity and importance of this doctrine we might remember what Karl Barth wrote in the foreword to the first volume of his *Church Dogmatics*: "I regard the analogy of being as *the* invention of the Anti-Christ, and think that *on account of it* one cannot become a Catholic. In saying this I venture at the same time to rate all other reasons one might have against becoming a Catholic as myopic and trivial."

The old sun still exerts a gravitational pull that the fiercest of wanderers still feel the need to resist.

More than this, I believe that Barth has actually not here fully identified the thing that *he* should regard as the Anti-Christ, i.e., the destructive enemy of the "true religion" that he supposes Protestantism to be. The real Anti-Christ for Barth, as for Luther before him, would be the *combination* of the doctrine of analogy with respect to the biblical honorifics addressed to God *with* the view that there is a terminology, namely, that of metaphysics, in which we can speak univocally of the finite and the Infinite, of the creature and the Creator. This is the kind of view that Aquinas exhibits when he characterizes God as identical with *Ipsum Esse*. Clearly the identification of God with *Ipsum Esse* is not intended by Aquinas to be analogy.

In this sense, Heidegger is a close follower of Luther, at least when it comes to his (Heidegger's) excoriation of metaphysics or "onto-theology."

What would be truly disconcerting for these thinkers (Luther, Barth, and even in a certain way Heidegger) would be the use of the terminology of an inchoate onto-theology by God when describing himself. But then there is Exodus 3:14–15.

cage. Analogy is located between these two extremes, as when, in Aristotle's examples, we refer to a human being and an image of one as both animals, or speak of a man and a regimen of exercise as both healthy.

For Aquinas, the use of the Divine "names," that is, predicates expressing the honorific attributes of God, cannot be univocal as between their application to God and their application to creatures. Consider the claim that God is wise. Those creatures who are wise, are wise accidentally; as it were, they have their wisdom added to their essence or nature. By contrast, because God is *a se* and accordingly simple, God *is* his Wisdom. That is why he can be said to be wise. The same holds for all the divine attributes. So Aquinas thinks that since what makes true the predication of an attribute of God will be so different from what makes true the corresponding predication made of creatures, the respective predications cannot be univocal. (An inference worthy of examination, but in another context.)

However, if we say that the corresponding predicates are applied only *equivocally* to God and his creatures, we thereby sever ourselves from any meaningful purpose in our talk of the nature of God. All we can do is follow Maimonides and talk negatively of God, and perhaps apply the official honorifics, although it will then be entirely unclear what the point of continuing to do that is.

As against this rather sterile *via negativa*, the whole ambition of Thomistic theology is to reconcile the transcendence of God with some degree of cognitive availability of the Divine, so that God could be a coherent object of religious thought and talk, and of feeling and prayer. Short of this cognitive accessibility, Maimonides must have been right to suggest that linguistic representation of God's nature is as misleading and idolatrous as any graven image of God. But where do we go from there; how do we even make a place for the coherence of the idea of God's self-revelation?

There are many strands in Thomas's treatment of analogy. Here is one of them, highlighted in a way that might indeed obscure other, very significant, strands. Thomas's treatment of analogy turns on the relationship between God and his creatures, in particular God's being the source of their existence and their essences, and his being the eminent exemplar of each of their perfections. On the epistemological side, on the side of our developing knowledge, we begin by learning what "wisdom" and all the other predications that express perfections mean as they are applied to creatures. But on the ontological side (and here is the crucial quasi-Platonic reasoning in Aquinas's account) such perfections must have their highest exemplars or forms. These highest examples or forms are the ontological ground of the respective perfection in creatures.

Now, Aquinas tells us, it is God that has these perfections to the highest degree. He is the highest exemplar for each of them. So when we say that God is wise, we are saying something that is made true by the fact that God is the eminent "cause" or ideal form of wisdom in all those creatures who are said to be wise. As Aquinas himself puts it, whatever wisdom we attribute to creatures, preexists in God—and "eminently," that is, in a more excellent and higher way.[6] However, in saying that God is wise, we are not just saying that God is the eminent cause of wisdom in creatures, for that would be a literal predication of a relational property of God, and not an analogical predication of an attribute of God. To predicate an attribute of God is always to predicate a perfection of God, and we can do that only by way of an analogy with the corresponding perfection found in creatures. So, when we consider the source of our knowledge of wisdom or goodness, God is said to be wise or good in a posterior or secondary way, with the prior sense coming from our understanding of the wisdom and goodness of some of his creatures. But ontologically, God's goodness and wisdom and other perfections are primary. God is Goodness, and he is Wisdom, and creatures get to be good or wise by participating in, by exemplifying, his Goodness and Wisdom.

Thomas's quasi-Platonic reasoning itself suggests that there must be a transcendental analogue in God of the corresponding perfection found in creatures. And it is tempting to think that a nonnegotiable part of any positive theology like Thomas's is to provide some reasonable gloss on the analogical basis in the Divine of the predications that structure our thought and feeling about him.

---

6. See *Summa Theologica* 1.13.2, "Whether Any Name Can Be Applied to God Substantially?"

Thomas himself appears to give in to this temptation when he explains God's perfect goodness in terms of God's being ultimately desirable. Since something is said to be good because it is properly desirable, God can be understood as good in a preeminent way, for he is the proper object of the whole desire-based orientation of his creatures.

In this way, giving some gloss on the transcendental analogue of the creaturely perfections that we predicate "by analogy" of God provides some determinate and distinctive content to each of the Divine Names.

The doctrine of analogy should not be seen as a quaint fixation of a bygone age. It is of profound theological import, for it provides a semantic and cognitive framework for any positive thought about God. What is unclear, however, is whether the doctrine of analogy really fits with the other centerpiece of Thomas's theology of Existence Itself, the identity theory of the Divine Nature. For at the end of the day, and precisely because an analogy seems to be a comparative relation between two things, we still seem inclined to say the following:

Albert Schweitzer's goodness must have something in common with God's goodness, even if it is only that there is a certain analogy between them, an analogy that does not hold between Schweitzer's existence and God's goodness.

Albert Schweitzer's existence must have something in common with God's existence, even if it is only that there is a certain analogy between them, an analogy that does not hold between Schweitzer's goodness and God's existence.

Unless remarks like these are true, we will be speaking only *equivocally* of "goodness" or "existence" when we apply such terms to God and to his creatures. But these remarks entail that God's goodness is not identical to God's existence, for different things stand in the relation of analogy to them.[7]

---

7. Notice that this argument for the nonidentity of God's attributes goes through even if we take seriously the Thomistic thought that all such relations of analogy are "really" grounded in our thought about God.

If I have not distorted Thomas's intentions too much, we have here a profound flaw in Thomas's profound theology of Existence Itself; Thomas's identity theory of God's nature is at odds with any good theory of analogical predication, any theory that will not in the end make divine predication, in effect, *equivocal.*

The paradox of the Highest One returns: any differentiated knowledge of the Highest One's nature will imply that this nature is complex, so that the Highest One is not *a se,* and so not the First in the order of being, and so is not, in fact, the Highest One.

We cannot rest content with that paradox. Either the very idea of the Highest One is incoherent, or at least completely beyond us, as in the doctrine of Maimonides, or the argument from the Highest One's being the source of reality, the First Being, to the simplicity of the Highest One is flawed.

What is missing in the tradition of argument from aseity to the identity theory of the divine nature is the idea of a *dependent* aspect or constituent. Not every whole made up of distinct parts is ontologically subordinate to those parts. For the parts may themselves essentially depend on the whole they make up.

And this is a point that not only preserves the coherence of Thomas's notion of God as Existence Itself; it also preserves the coherence of a more inclusive successor of that notion.

Existents as Dependent Aspects of Existence Itself

There is an experience—some would say it is a metaphysical experience; some would say it is inchoately religious—of being, as Ludwig Wittgenstein once put it, *absolutely safe.* (Wittgenstein appears to have had experiences of this sort when, as a medical orderly in the trenches in World War I, he was in danger of being shot, gassed, or blown up. Marcus Aurelius, another man of the trenches, describes a similar experience in his *Meditations.*) Part of the content of this experience, as opposed to the content of its subsequent interpretation, is that no matter what happens, everything that is fundamentally precious will remain intact. That content supervenes upon a distinctive way of sensing one's environment. In the experience of feeling absolutely safe, every-thing in one's sensory field is presented as a manifestation of something that remains the same despite its various transformations into the things that come into being and pass away. Moreover, on the side of introspection or inner perception, one is given to oneself as just another such manifestation, one whose passing away will leave intact everything that is fundamentally precious. It is, if you like, an experience of ordi-nary existents as dependent aspects of something else, as modes or modifications of that something else, which itself always remains. Yet to leave it at that is a quite desiccating analysis of the experience; part of the content of the experience is immense joy at the endless preserva-tion of what is fundamentally precious.

Adhering to our method, we should set aside, at least for now, the question of whether the experience of being absolutely safe is *veridical*, and just try to characterize the content of the experience. The content, as set out above, seems coherent, at least if we can make sense of a dependent part or aspect.

Here are some examples of the idea of a dependent part. A specific tooth, a tooth that grew in a specific person's mouth, could not have originally grown in another person's mouth. Its actual origin enters into *what it is to be* that very tooth; that origin would have to be men-tioned in any full account of, as the philosophers say, the essence of the tooth. The tooth is a genuine part of the person's body, yet it is ontologically dependent on the person's body. Or consider a "sideways" part, the upper half of a specific person's body, not considered at a time, but considered over time—as it were the *variable* upper half of that person's body, a part that increases in size by half of any increase in the size of the person's body as a whole.[8] The identity of the person's body enters into what it is to be that part. You could not give a full account of the essence of the variable upper half of a person's body without mentioning the body of the person in question. The variable upper half of a person's body is a dependent part of that body; it is ontologically dependent on the person's body. Likewise for the variable lower half of a person's body. So a person's body considered over time

8. An example of Kit Fine's.

could be divided into two dependent parts, its variable upper half and its variable lower half. Although these parts exhaust the body in question, they are ontologically dependent on it. Here we have a division of the temporally extended body into dependent parts.

With the idea of a dependent part in hand, we can return to the arguments from aseity to simplicity, and from simplicity to the identity theory of the Divine Nature. Aquinas's canonical form of the argument that the First Being, the absolute source of reality, must be simple—

> Every composite thing is posterior to its components and dependent on them. But, as was shown above, God is the First Being.

—misses an ontological option, namely, that of the dependent part or component, which is posterior to, that is, ontologically dependent upon, the whole it makes up.

So the First Being *can be complex,* and its attributes need not be identical. And there is, therefore, no need to go all the way to purely negative treatment of divine predication.

This small clarifying point in ontology, the existence of dependent parts, has a number of consequences for the understanding of the Highest One. (For example, pace Jean-Luc Marion, we need not completely cross out Being in order to make room for the Christian revelation that God is Love.[9] We need only displace Being a little.)

AN ALTERNATIVE TO THE THOMISTIC INTERPRETATION OF THE HIGHEST ONE

Once we understand that complexity can enter into the nature of the Highest One, we may avail ourselves of an alternative to the traditional theistic interpretation of the Highest One as utterly transcendent, and so changeless, timeless, and unaffected by the world of ordinary existents.

Compare these two conflicting identifications:

9. See Jean-Luc Marion, *God without Being* (University of Chicago Press, 1991).

The Highest One = Existence Itself.

The Highest One = the outpouring of Existence Itself by way of
its exemplification in ordinary existents.

The first identification is the traditional Thomistic identification, and it makes the Highest One "impassable," that is, inherently unaffected by its exemplifications. Existence Itself does not change; it is not a process but an *eidos*, the eminent exemplar of all existence. As such, it is self-complete, and so not at all put at risk by way of anything that happens in the world of ordinary existents. When we ask why Existence Itself is exemplified (by something not itself), nothing in the nature of Existence Itself seems to account for this.

Perhaps the most distinctive part of Christian revelation is that the Highest One is by its nature Love, a revelation concretely presented in such details as the intimate way in which Jesus addresses the Creator as *Abba* or "Dada."

To say that God is Love must, of course, be predication by analogy, for it is the Highest One who is here being described. And there is indeed an analogy between self-giving love and the outpouring of Existence Itself by way of its exemplification in ordinary existents. But relative to Existence Itself this outpouring of exemplification seems like a further contingent fact; for Existence Itself may or may not be exemplified (by something other than itself), and either way it would remain self-complete. Whatever can be said of the essential nature of Existence Itself would have to hold in either contingency, and so, on the Thomistic identification of the Highest One with Existence Itself, the analogical basis for describing Existence Itself as Love does not lie in the essential nature of the Highest One. This seems a fatal flaw in the traditional identification. Here, at least, the familiar gibe against the "god of the philosophers," namely, that it is sterile relative to the god of faith, seems well-placed.

The second identification does not share this flaw. The Highest One is a certain kind of activity that could be analogically described as Loving, for it is the self-giving outpouring of Existence Itself by way of its exemplification in existents. On this second identification, the Highest One is not Being, and not any ordinary existent; it is Being's Self-

Giving. It is this Self-Giving in which we "live and move and have our being," as Paul put it on Mars Hill (Acts 17:28), thereby quoting the Stoic poet Epimenides.

That is an argument for the second identification of the Highest One from crucial aspects of Christian revelation. As such, the argument is localized within one tradition of theism. Can we find an argument that each tradition might endorse?

Chapter 8

Process Panentheism

In all theistic traditions the Highest One is taken to be perfectly good. Now in naive atheism and its counterpart naive theodicy, the attempt to justify the ways of God the Benefactor to his unsatisfied client, man, the analogical nature of this honorific predication is ignored, and we are supposed to face such worrying inconsistencies as this:

> If the Highest One is perfectly good, and all-powerful, then there should be no evil in the world that is not necessary for a greater good. Yet there is much evil in the world that is not necessary for a greater good.

The Highest One is here being asked to be good in the way that a patron or benefactor is good, he is being asked to favor the ways of human beings or suffering animals, and he is being found wanting in all this. Given *this* conception of what the Highest One's Goodness would consist in, the only honest response would be to conclude that he is either not good or not powerful. The present thought is that the central issue of theodicy, the problem of unnecessary evil, arises only with a conception of Divine Goodness that expresses the idolatrous longing for a useful god, one who will favor us with something *other than* his own self-revelation. Theodicy is not only in that way a form of intellectual idolatry; it is based on a naive theory of the meaning of divine predication.

Aquinas explains the goodness of God as God's being eminently desirable, desirable in a way that is more complete and coherent than the way in which any other object of desire could be desirable. Being maximally desirable, God can be said (analogically, of course) to rightly command the total affirmation of his nature by our wills.

However, that analogue of goodness gets no foothold at all in Existence Itself. How could an unchanging *eidos* be maximally desirable? Desiring it or affirming it would be like desiring or affirming the number 2. On the other hand, the outpouring of Existence Itself by way of its exemplification in ordinary existents seems well suited to command total affirmation by one's will. It is a process that makes up all of reality, and, arguably, to affirm this process and thoroughly identify with it is to truly love God.

As it stands, that last observation is premature, for we have omitted something essential in our identification of the Highest One, something to which each of the major monotheisms testifies. The common vision of Judaism, Christianity, and Islam is that the Highest One does not want us to be just *in* him, as elements in his reality; the Highest One wants us to be *with* him. That is, he seeks us out by way of his revelation and his prophets in order to lead us to participate in his own self-disclosure. This, according to the common vision, is the whole point of the outpouring of Existence Itself. If you like, it is, according to the common vision, the *will* of the Highest One to disclose himself. (It must be admitted that the common vision is often wildly distorted by idolatrous elements, such as the vengeful fantasies of the End Times, and the literally sexed-up Feasts of Heaven.)

So our interpretive identification of the Highest One is more complete if expressed this way:

> The Highest One = the outpouring of Existence Itself by way of its exemplification in ordinary existents for the sake of the self-disclosure of Existence Itself.

So far, this is meant only to express a familiar theme, found in the traditions of each of the major monotheisms, the theme of outpouring and return by way of our entering into the inner life of the Highest One. Compare Paul (Romans 11:36): "from him and through him and *to him* are all beings."

The Analogy of Logos

Benedict, following the opening of the Gospel of John, "In the beginning was the λόγος," speaks of God as Logos or Reason. He insists that

there is an analogy between God's Reason and ours, and that this analogy enables us to discern what God as Reason could not allow or require—for example, violent coercion in the name of faith.

> [B]etween God and us, between his eternal Creator Spirit and our
> created reason there exists a real analogy, in which—as the Fourth
> Lateran Council in 1215 stated—unlikeness remains infinitely
> greater than likeness, yet not to the point of abolishing analogy
> and its language. God does not become more divine when we
> push him away from us in a sheer, impenetrable voluntarism;
> rather, the truly divine God is the God who has revealed himself
> as *logos*.

What is Logos? The notion appears first in the fragments of Heracli-
tus, where the Logos is a preeminent ordering principle that governs
all things, a principle that is rational in the sense of meeting the highest
standards of intelligibility, even though the full grasp of its nature is
beyond us. The Stoics, by the third century BCE, had developed the
original Heraclitean idea into a conception of the Logos as a rational
divine power that orders and directs the universe. This part of the idea
of the Logos may live on in the contemporary notion of the body of
natural laws, which our best science may partly reveal, and which governs all that happens in the universe.

But how could what we now think of the totality of the laws of nature, the ordering principle of all that happens, also be called "reason"
and "the Word," as the more familiar translations of the opening of
John's Gospel have it? How could the Highest One just *be* the laws of
nature? Surely when we speak of the Highest One as Logos, we are not
simply identifying the Highest One with the totality of such laws. For
this would mean that basic science and theology have the very same
subject matter.

In thinking of the Highest One as Logos we would do better by conceiving of Logos as the principle of intelligibility of all that happens, a
kind of preeminent rational intelligibility whose ends are served by the
operations of the laws of nature.

What are the ends of the Highest One? The reference to "the Word"
at the beginning of the Gospel of John suggests that the Logos as preeminent rational intelligibility is essentially communicated in the un-

folding of the universe and in human history, and it is because of this that preeminent rational intelligibility deserves the name of "intelligible speech" or "Word." So in the revelation of the Highest One as Logos, the Highest One is revealed as communicating or disclosing himself in creation and to us.

Of course, in thus talking of the ends of the Highest One, we can only be talking either idolatrously or analogically. The Highest One does not deliberate about outcomes. It does not choose, set a course, and then adjust events to keep things on that course. The Highest One is not a Great Controller who intervenes in worldly events for the sake of his consciously formulated ends. He is not another efficient cause, alongside the physical causes.

Why, then, speak of the ends, or the will, of the Highest One at all? What makes the use of the teleological idiom at all helpful here is the revealed idea that the Highest One is not just the source of existence, but is continuously and cumulatively disclosing himself in the universe and in history, and that this is what the universe and human history are for the sake of. This itself is an analogical interpretation of reality and history, one forced on believers by the details of monotheistic revelation. The teleological idiom expresses one form of the feeling of our radical dependence on the Highest One, and of our hope to return to him. This is the content of the common monotheistic revelation of God as Alpha and Omega, as our ontological source and final end.

I hope to make more sense of this below, after an examination of what we must add to the natural realm of efficient causes in order to make sense of disclosure, even as it occurs in ordinary conscious awareness.

Process Panentheism

Given our method, it is not for us to dispute or defend the view that the common monotheistic revelation of God as Alpha and Omega, as ontological source and final end, is a *veridical* revelation. And anyway, it is very unclear what it would be to *argue* about that. Rather our method directs us to explicate the content of the revelation and test its content against the touchstone of idolatry. Could it be the Highest One who is thus revealed?

Here at last we do seem to have a view of God that is at least purged of the *familiar* idolatrous elements. One sign of this is that the God thus revealed offers us no special levers to push or pull for our own worldly advantage; so we can hardly be said to be dealing with a projection of our own desires for a kind of control over our lives that eludes our ordinary human powers. Another sign is that his "will"—or more precisely the analogue of will in him that we are able to make clear to ourselves—is outpouring and self-disclosure, something we can recognize as the ideal prototype of our highest ideal of love. Here at last, we *may* have caught a glimpse of the Highest One.

The glimpse allows for a theological clarification in our thought and talk of the Highest One. We can distinguish two strands of theological reflection concerning the Highest One: for want of better names, "classical theism" and "panentheism."

The God of classical theism is the utterly transcendent unmoved mover, a being totally self-complete without creation, an eternal one, that is, a being outside of time, who remains unchanged by creation and the course it takes in time. The world is in no way part of the nature or essence of such a God. This God might well be identified with Existence Itself, the transcendent prototype of all individual "existences," as in the theology of Aquinas.

By contrast, the defining motto of panentheism is "God in all, and all in God." Panentheism should be carefully distinguished from the *pantheistic identification* of God and the natural realm. Against such a pantheistic identification, the panentheist will assert that God is partly *constituted* by the natural realm, in the sense that his activity is manifest in and through natural processes *alone*. But his reality goes beyond what is captured by the purely scientific description of all the events that make up the natural realm. Nothing in the natural realm lies outside God, and God reveals himself in the natural realm by disclosing in religious experience an ultimate form of the world, one that is in no way at odds with the form of the natural realm disclosed by science:

that is, a causal realm closed under natural law. The identification broached earlier—

> The Highest One = the outpouring of Existence Itself by way of its exemplification in ordinary existents for the purpose of the self-disclosure of Existence Itself

—characterizes that ultimate form of reality, and thereby expresses a type of panentheism. It identifies God with a universal process understood as outpouring and self-disclosure. Here, God is no longer in the category of substance, as in traditional theology, but in the category of activity. As such, God is radically at risk in the world; he needs us just as we need him, for we are the potential sites of his self-disclosure.

Recall the inner truth of the ban on idolatry: the requirement that our worship be directed to the Highest One, the One most worthy of worship. Worship, in the relevant sense in which idolatry is perverse worship, was understood to involve the expression of fealty or devotion to the will or purpose of the object of worship. Both Existence Itself and the outpouring and self-disclosure of Existence Itself can be said, analogically, to have a will or purpose, namely, the very outpouring and self-disclosure in question, as in the ostensibly revealed theme of Alpha and Omega, creation and return.

The choice between classical theism and panenetheism is, if you like, a choice between a first principle and the expressive activity of that first principle. The latter is the more inclusive object of worship, for it includes not only the serene perfections of Existence Itself, but the perfections inherent in its universal act of outpouring and self-disclosure. In that sense, panentheism appears to provide a more suitable theological description of the Highest One.[1]

---

1. My theological readers will be more than familiar with the precursors of this idea, in particular Alfred North Whitehead's *Process and Reality: An Essay in Cosmology*, ed. David Ray Griffin and Donald W. Sherburne (Free Press, 1979), and Charles Hartshorne's *A Natural Theology for Our Time* (Open Court, 1967). See also Arthur Peacocke, *All That Is* (Fortress Press, 2007), and the articles in Philip Clayton and Arthur Peacocke, *In Whom We Live and Move and Have Our Being* (Erdman's Publishing, 2004). John W. Cooper has provided a very useful overview of panentheistic thought in his recent *Panenetheism: The Other God of the Philosophers—From Plato to the Present* (Baker Academic Press, 2006).

THE SELF-DISCLOSURE OF EXISTENCE ITSELF

Classical theism, with its emphasis on the eternal, perfect, self-complete creator set over against a changing, imperfect, and uncompleted creation, recapitulates the dualism of Being and Becoming, and leaves God without any "skin" in the created world. Christian doctrine understands the Incarnation—Jesus' being both God and man—as having overcome this primary ontological dualism. Yet despite (or is it because of?) the ingenious devices of official Christology, such as the suggestion that Jesus had two minds, a finite mind filled with the limited outlook of a first-century Galilean, and a separate, infinite mind that knew all, the doctrine of the Incarnation simply looks like the *reassertion* that, in Jesus at least, the dualism of perfect being and arduous becoming is overcome.[2]

Process theology, and, in particular, the identification of the Highest One with the all-inclusive process of the outpouring of Existence Itself into existents for the sake of self-disclosure, makes the old Self-Complete Being of classical theology just one pole of God, the activity of outpouring and self-disclosure, and to that extent overcomes the dualism between being and becoming. The incarnation of the Divine is ubiquitous.

Moreover, in its emphasis on the self-disclosure of Existence Itself, our identification of God with this process brings to center stage the very theme that Martin Heidegger found to be repressed in the Platonic and Aristotelian treatment of Being, and which therefore remains repressed in any "inner rapprochement between Greek Philosophy and Biblical Faith." This repressed theme is the theme of Being-making-itself-present. Heidegger's suggestion was that the repression of this theme in the history of metaphysics can be understood as a symptom, on the side of thought, of a systematic retreat from a lived sense of Being-making-itself-present, and so—*we* might say—from the numi-

2. For a careful philosophical exploration of the two minds thesis, see Thomas V. Morris, *The Logic of God Incarnate* (Cornell University Press, 1986).

nous and the holy. It is this "forgetfulness of Being" that allows us to replace reverence for reality with an instrumental attitude toward our environment, and toward our own lives, so that they become means to power and advantage.

That is, on its face, another philosophical allegory of the Fall of Humanity. The allegory can be extended to encompass the emergence of the gods and the appearance of claimants to the title of "the One God." By taking for granted, or "forgetting," the numinous and already holy reality of Being-making-itself-present, our fundamental ways of thinking about the world and of living in it have been formed on an impious basis, and so over time we are led to a view of reality as only a realm in which power and advantage may be pursued. Into this dedivinized world, the gods appear as localized pockets of the numinous and the holy. When they reveal themselves, a circumscribed sense of the holy returns. But because this is experienced as the exceptional, set aside from the mainstream of life as we experience it, there is a constant falling-away from the perceived demands of the gods.

It is, then, no surprise that the novelty of the Almighty but Jealous god eventually appears; he is a god who rightly anticipates our habitual falling-away, and so he constantly threatens us with retaliation if we do so. He is a god who will not let us go. Thus Yahweh, like the other gods, arrives at a certain point in the history of neglect of the holiness of reality; and like the other gods, he plays a conspiratorial role in continuing that neglect, by offering us a kind of favored treatment that is very hard to refuse.

The emergence of Allah, who demands that we continually bring him to mind in all our thoughts and deeds, can be understood as another way of coping with the dedivinization of the world. Allah is the focus of the grand attempt to redivinize the world; he insists that we continually remind ourselves of his transcendence and submit ourselves to it.

But was the world originally holy by way of its being the artifact of a Transcendent Divine Creator? Could the holiness of the world not instead consist just in the sheer givenness of the world—that is, in its existence and disclosure—so that true piety requires that we be willing to let go of anthropomorphic concepts of God, which, however they might be idealized and transcendentalized, obscure the true nature of the Divine?

The Problem Is with the Pantheon

Focus for a moment on the long historical journey from polytheism to henotheism and then on to monotheism, and consider what it looks like, in the wake of the foregoing. First there is the polytheist's pantheon of gods—think of the many gods of ancient Egypt—which from the reductive psychological point of view might be described as the product of our natural tendency to impute agency to various natural forces. Then henotheism emerges, in one or another form, with the identification of one of the gods in the pantheon as the top god, the god of gods. Compare the Egyptian cult of Amon Ra or the early versions of the religion of Yahweh. (Is henotheism typically the expression of the triumph of one sector of the priestly class over the others?)

Then monotheism, relying essentially on the rhetoric of idolatrousness, clears the pantheon of the lesser gods, leaving only the top god as the one god. That kind of monotheism is just the limiting case of polytheism. Its one god is just the last remaining god of a polytheistic pantheon. Of course, the last remaining god can then be invested with many of the virtues of the expelled gods. But here we have no deep religious transformation either of the last remaining god, or of his adherents. If it was idolatrous to worship the remaining god when he was one among the pantheon of gods, why does it cease to be idolatrous just because the other gods have been cleared from the pantheon? Is this why the original ban on idolatry, in Exodus 20, is itself refracted through an idolatrous prism?

Panentheism breaks with this cycle: the problem was with the pantheon, and *not with its number of inhabitants*. The pantheon is the temple of spiritual materialism; there are the deities to be placated, and here, so the priests tell us, are the required methods of supplication.

A religion that embodied panentheism would not be a religion of placation or supplication of the last god remaining from what once was a pantheon of gods. It would instead be a return to the God before the gods, namely, Being continually making itself present on the holy ground we have always in fact inhabited.

Recall the large-scale structural defects of human life, which include arbitrary suffering, the decay of corrosive aging, our profound ignorance of our condition, the isolation produced by ordinary self-involvement, the vulnerability of everything we cherish to time and chance, and, finally, to untimely death. The religious or redeemed life is one in which these large-scale defects are somehow finally healed or addressed or rendered irrelevant, so that faith in the importance of goodness not only remains but is strengthened, even in the face of these defects.

There is a characteristically idolatrous substitute for genuine faith in the importance of goodness even in the face of death and the other large-scale structural defects; namely, belief in speculative propositions about the afterlife, the other world, and so forth. The other world has been and continues to be the font of idolatry. We are promised that so long as we placate the right god, we will have another life in which the large-scale defects of this life are not just redeemed but *removed*. We are promised that if only we make the appropriate supplications, we will awake from death into a life without death, without suffering, struggle, or effort, a life in which our desires are always satisfied. But there can be no such human life; any such life would be by its very nature not our life.[3]

The promise of the other world is a false promise, which could be made only by an idolatrous religion that aims not at transforming us spiritually but at pandering to us in our untransformed condition. Everything depends on the distinction between an imagined other life in which the large-scale defects are miraculously removed, and redemption in this life—that is, a transformed outlook in which those defects are somehow overcome.

---

3. See, for example, the heroically explicit discussion of the afterlife provided by Marilyn McCord Adams in her wonderful work *Christ and Horrors* (Cambridge University Press, 2004). That McCord Adams's kind of afterlife is not *accessible* to us, either by way of the postmortem survival of the soul or by way of the bodily or the psychological criteria of personal identity, is one thesis of *Surviving Death*.

It is by encouraging its adherents to attend to the self-disclosure of Being, rather than placate another god, that panentheism distinguishes itself from the idolatrous religions.

Salvation, understood as the goal of religious or spiritual life, is a new orientation that authentically addresses the large-scale defects of human life, and thereby provides a reservoir of energy otherwise dissipated in denial of, and resistance to, necessary suffering. Salvation, so understood, is a new orientation, a new form of life, which finds itself as the expression and the subject of Divine self-disclosure.

Chapter 9

Panentheism, Not Pantheism

DISTINGUISHING PANENTHEISM AND PANTHEISM

What does the difference between panentheism and pantheism come to, exactly?

Can it not be made to seem a trivial difference, in the following way? Both share the same ontology; for both, it seems, all that exists is the natural realm, but whereas pantheism identifies God with the natural realm, panentheism replaces the "is" of identity with the "is" of constitution and finds that God is wholly constituted by the natural realm.

Compare the following, *in itself* fairly trivial, dispute in philosophy. Kripke claims that water = H_2O. Other thinkers point out that H_2O can be found in a variety of nonidentical states, that is, as water, as ice, as snow, and as steam; so that the better thing to say is that (pure) water is wholly constituted by H_2O, as is (pure) ice, snow, and steam. They differ in their manifest form; but they have the very same material constitution, as is reveal by chemistry.[1]

It is important to see that the distinction between panentheism and pantheism cannot be usefully drawn in this way if the natural realm is all there is. If the natural realm were all that existed, then the natural sciences would reveal not only the ultimate constitution of the world *but also its overarching form*. All that exists would be the realm of law-governed efficient causation, holding among the basic items disclosed by the natural sciences, along with the patterns of material constitution that take us from those basic items to the items that make up the manifest world. That just is the natural realm, and it would be the world, the whole of reality, on the supposition at hand.

---

1. For a development of this view, see "Constitution Is Not Identity," *Mind* 101 (1991), and "Manifest Kinds," *Journal of Philosophy* 94 (1997).

That is, if all that existed were the natural realm, then there would be a consistent but quite eccentric view to the effect that

God = the natural realm

and this would deserve the name of pantheism. But there would be no room even for a consistent panentheism to the effect that

God is wholly constituted by the natural realm.

For *ex hypothesi* there would be no more comprehensive form than the form of the natural realm. We would not be able to say, "God is wholly constituted by the natural realm and is numerically distinct from the natural realm in virtue of having this different form." On the hypothesis that the natural realm is all that there is, talk of God has little point.

But did we not commit ourselves to this hypothesis by endorsing legitimate naturalism, as expressed, say, in some improved variant of Davidson's thesis of the nomological character of causation? No, we precisely did not. Legitimate naturalism is not the thesis that only the natural realm exists. That is the thesis of scientism. Legitimate naturalism is the view that the domain of the natural sciences is complete on its own terms: every causal transaction ultimately consists in some utterly natural process, for example, mass-energy transfer. There are no gods of the gaps. That is the extent of legitimate naturalism, the naturalism that expresses proper respect for the discoveries of the natural sciences.

Yes, but what else could there be, besides the natural realm? What is it that falls outside of the domain of the natural sciences?

Some panentheists have answered: spirit, mind, consciousness. They then went on to suggest that God may stand to the natural realm in a way that is analogous to the way in which the human mind stands to the body.

Let me say straight out that this is a dead end. Theoretically, the concept of a nonnatural mental realm is bankrupt. And spiritually, the very idea of mind is a manifestation of our fallen condition, the condition in which we still encounter the natural realm as merely THERE as the object of our representations, and so as just a series of opportunities and obstacles in the promotion of our self-will. The very idea of consciousness as a subjective mental phenomenon is a kind of blindness to the gift, a profoundly impious theft, an attempt to appropriate to oneself the source of intelligibility.

The meaning of these strange sayings will become clear by the end of this chapter.

What *else* exists then? What is there in addition to the natural realm, such that when we put it together with the natural realm we then have something whose overarching form could motivate serious talk of God?[2]

The realm of sense, the realm of that in virtue of which things are intelligible: this is the realm we need to explore in order to work our way inside a serious panentheism.

Unfortunately, in defending the autonomy of the realm of sense, we shall have to engage in argumentative trench warfare with the dominant philosophical conception of intelligibility, a conception that, almost as a matter of reflex, treats intelligibility as a mental phenomenon and then attempts to reduce this mental phenomenon to a transaction in the natural realm by way of essential reliance on the bogus notion of natural representation.

So now we shall have to do some more philosophy.

If the reader has no taste for philosophical trench warfare, or believes (with some plausibility) that it can at most produce temporary and Pyrrhic victories, I invite him or her to skip ahead with the correct thought that this will be a no doubt fallible input into our admittedly fallible conception of the Highest One.

PRESENCE

According to Martin Heidegger, at least as I am inclined to read that difficult writer, the very idea of the natural realm is a certain sort of abstraction, one that seems as if it could exhaust everything there is only because of a historic forgetfulness of Being-making-itself-present.

Heidegger claims that an important intellectual symptom of this forgetfulness of Being-making-itself-present is the centrality in the history

---

2. Talk of "addition" should not be taken too seriously here. Once we understand the larger whole that includes the other realm, the natural realm will appear as a certain sort of abstraction from that whole.

of metaphysics and theology (so-called onto-theology) of a secondary conception of truth as correspondence between a proposition and a fact, to the exclusion of a primary conception of truth as disclosure of the very materials, the very topics of thought and talk, that make up thinkable propositions. Only because beings are disclosed to us do we have access to the propositions that are the bearers of truth understood as correspondence to the facts; without such disclosure the very propositions that are the content of our thought and talk, and of our scientific theories of the natural realm, would not be accessible to us. So truth-as-disclosure is prior to truth-as-correspondence.

Regarding disclosure as *a kind of truth*, rather than a precondition for grasping the bearers of truth-as-correspondence, seems optional. Perhaps Heidegger's reason for this assimilation is that he wants to urge upon us his characteristically overimaginative etymology of "aletheia," the Greek word for truth, as having its origins in "a-letheia"; by keeping in mind Lethe, the mythic river of forgetfulness or concealment, Heidegger finds himself able to translate this word as *Unverborgenheit*, that is, "unconcealment" or disclosure.

Whether or not disclosure is *a kind of truth*, it is what gives content to all experience and thought. And the disclosure of Being, including the variety of ways in which individual beings present, is a fact that is as primordial or basic as the reality of individual existents.

I mention Heidegger because I believe he is right, at least about this: the presence of Being, its giving itself as the content of intelligible experience and thought, is very difficult to bring into view. This is especially so because our whole way of thinking about mind and reality, and hence about presence or disclosure, is conditioned by a misplaced idea of representation. We must spend some time rooting out that idea in order to clarify the notion of presence and its relation to Objective Mind, and to the Divine Mind.

PRESENCE AS DISCLOSURE

So our topic is presence, the variety of ways in which items, be they objects, qualities, or whatever, disclose some aspect of their nature. Perhaps the best way to bring presence into view is to begin with perception. When one sees one's dogs running in the front yard, the whole content of the perceptual experience is of the dogs and their running being present in a certain way, a way that discloses something of the nature of the dogs and their running. There the dogs are, immediately available as objects of attention and demonstration, and as topics of one's further thought and talk. The experience is not made up of mental stuff, whatever that might be. Ectoplasm, ideas, sense data? It is made up of the dogs and the manners in which they present.

The same could be said of one's bodily sensational states such as pain and nausea; in those states certain qualities are presented as part of a quasi-three-dimensional body image, as it were a volume of felt quality. THERE those qualities are, immediately available as objects of thought and talk.

As well as perceptual and bodily sensational presence there is also intellectual presence, where what is made present are objects of judgment and belief, namely, propositions whose truth or falsity determines the truth or falsity of the judgment or belief in question. Because most thought involves the exploitation of conventional systems of signs, propositions are typically made present in thought by way of the meanings conventionally associated with the signs employed.[3] Thanks to this, THERE those propositions are, available as objects of attention, as objects of manipulation in reasoning, and as things to be judged true or false, and believed, or disbelieved.

Once presence comes into view, something more can be said about perception, bodily sensation, and thought. Perceptual experiences, somatic experiences, and thoughts are individuated by the very items they present or make available, and by the ways in which they present or make available those items. My seeing my dogs running is not some state or event that just happens to be about my dogs, my feeling pain is not just some state or event that just happens to be directed upon pain, and my thinking that Vienna is delightful is not some state or event that just happens to concern Vienna. The connection between a state that makes something present and *what* it makes present is not

---

3. Which is not to say that the words, as they figure in my thoughts, are contingently related to their conventional meanings. The words that figure in my thoughts, figure as semantically interpreted words. So here, too, there is no room for a verbalized thought's turning out to be contingently related to the proposition it is directed at.

an accidental feature of that state. It enters into the essence of that state; it partly defines what it is to be that state.

As we will see, this means that there must be something wrong with thinking of such states as just consisting in representations of what they are about, representations that get to be *of* or *about* their targets because of some happy mix of relations like causation and descriptive matching. For those relations do not hold essentially of the things of which they happen to hold.

Is Being Almost Entirely Wasted?

On the standard view of the relation between consciousness and reality, most of being is absolutely wasted, for only an infinitesimally small fraction of what exists is ever present, that is, ever discloses or reveals some aspect of its nature. On this view, when the last individual consciousness ceases to be, the very local phenomenon of presence will end. The lights will have gone out, all over the universe, never to go on again.

This way of thinking about both the nature of reality and the nature of consciousness treats us as "Producers of Presence"—that is, beings whose psychological operations are the very preconditions of presence or disclosure. As a way of thinking, this stands almost unopposed in contemporary philosophy; that we are Producers of Presence is not even a *formulated* thesis, since it is treated as the most obvious common sense, a bedrock starting point.[4]

To find any sort of traditional alternative to it, you would have to turn back to Spinoza, or Maimonides, or Ibn Sina, or, better, to the

---

4. What was called the "Theory of Appearing" treated the perceptual case as an exception to the orthodoxy that we are Producers of Presence. It has recently been revived by William Alston in his "Back to the Theory of Appearing," *Nous* 33 (2002). The Theory of Appearing is appealing, but it is not the whole truth. It needs to be augmented with an adequate account of hallucination, and this in its turn will require the recognition that among the things that can appear are *objective* qualities and structures of these. See "The Obscure Object of Hallucination," *Philosophical Studies* 120 (2004), and the larger essay from which the present discussion is drawn, "Objectivity of Mind and the Objectivity of Our Minds," *Philosophy and Phenomenological Research* 66 (2007). Still, the Theory of Appearing is the closest precursor to what follows here. You would not go too far wrong by thinking of what follows as a grand generalization of the Theory of Appearing.

passage that influenced them all, namely, Aristotle's amazing lines on the Active Intellect in *De Anima*, book 3, chapter 5.

> [M]ind as we have described it is what it is by virtue of becoming all things, while there is another Mind which is what it is by virtue of making all things be present: this is a sort of positive state like light.

Only in such places do we find the idea of mind as thoroughly objective, and of presence as already fully actualized, independently of the psychological operations of particular human beings. In Aristotle, Ibn Sina, and Maimonides it is *intellectual* presence that is understood as already fully actualized; individual intellectual acts partake of this preexisting presence and *access* their contents from it.

I believe that a similar view can be made out when it comes to perceptual and bodily sensory presence. In fact, the very immediacy of perceptual experience provides one route to the idea of preexisting presence.

Opposed to the hypothesis that we are Producers of Presence is the hypothesis that we are, thanks to our distinctive sensibility, highly selective Samplers of Presence. On this hypothesis, Being is by its nature present; Being's fundamental activity is self-disclosure. All the modes of presentation of each existing thing, be they intellectual or sensory modes, all the possible *ways* of thinking and sensing each such thing, come into being with the things themselves, whether or not there are any individual minds to sample these modes of presentation, that is, to access them in individual mental acts.

UBIQUITOUS PRESENCE

Are we Producers or Samplers of Presence? Our verdict on that will determine our answer to the basic question of intentionality: How could an inner mental state of a person, something wholly constituted by his brain states, be *about* an item that exists independently of those states?

Here, in the face of this question, the almost universal conviction that we are Producers of Presence relies on an auxiliary hypothesis, the hypothesis of natural representation. Inner mental states, wholly constituted by their associated brain states, are natural representational states; they involve natural, as opposed to conventional, representations of items in the external environment.

The primal scene for the emergence of the idea of natural representation might be taken to be the scene inside the *camera obscura*, an optical device used in the early Renaissance in perspective-preserving drawing. (The *camera obscura* is first described by Leonardo da Vinci in his *Codex Atlanticus*, though *camerae obscurae* may have existed even as early as the tenth century.) The *camera obscura* is a dark box or chamber with a small aperture on one side. Light from an external scene passes through the aperture and strikes a specific part of the far wall of the dark chamber, projecting an inverted image of the external scene. Standing in the box, one can see the inverted image of the external scene, preserved in perspective. The artist can then trace the image in order to sketch the basis for a realistic painting of the scene.

The inverted image is a nonconventional or "natural" representation of the external scene. It is caused by the external scene in a particularly direct and salient way, and it resembles the scene in obvious ways. That is why it is useful as a template for a realistic painting of the scene.

At first, the further, and rather seductive, philosophical gloss on all this seems entirely innocent: it is *thanks* to this favorable mix of causation and resemblance that the inverted image gets to be *of* or *about* the scene external to the chamber. The same could be said of images in mirrors; they may be taken to be natural representations, which get to be of or about their originals thanks to a favorable mix of causation and resemblance.

So the dominating scheme of thought has it that the allegedly natural representational capacities of the brain also get to be *of* or *about* scenes in the external world, thanks to some favorable mix of causation and resemblance.

The hypothesis of natural representation appears to work smoothly with the unquestioned hypothesis that we are Producers of Presence. A scene in the external world causes one's brain to go into a certain natural representational state; that state is appropriately caused by the scene and in a certain way resembles it, perhaps via complex isomorphisms. That is why the state gets to be *of* the external scene. That scene becomes present, and this means present *to a subject,* because that subject has a natural representation of the scene caused in him by that very scene, a representation that is also in significant ways like the scene. Without such causal transactions and resembling natural representations nothing would be present. So the disappearance of brains and other systems that might be the sites of such natural representations means the end of presence. For, so the idea goes, without natural representations there is no presence.

Throughout contemporary philosophy and cognitive science we find the conviction that something like this *must be right,* even if the details have to undergo some revision in order to handle particular cases. How could it be otherwise?

AGAINST NATURAL REPRESENTATION

Yet even in the case of mirror images, or images on the walls of *camerae obscurae,* the hypothesis of natural representation seems misplaced. In fact, those images get to be *of* or *about* their originals because we *see them and treat them as of or about* their originals. This can shown by a double strategy of ringing the changes on causation and sifting through the claims to resemblance.

A scheme of mirrors and light filters might be added to the inside of a *camera obscura* so that an image appears anamorphically, and in colors complementary to those of its original. Is the image still a natural representation of its original, and, if so, has there not been a very significant change in the pattern of causation that led to its production? Whence the conviction that there must be some unifying description of such different patterns of causation, a description that could then be put forward as a necessary part of a set of sufficient conditions whereby one thing, a natural representation, is *of or about* another? Must there be a unifying description that could play this role? Isn't it likely that the various causal processes by which representational states are produced do not form a natural class?

So consider the Sudarium of Orvieto, taken by some to be the towel that Veronica offered to Christ on the road to Calvary to wipe his bloody face. Suppose for a moment that it contains, as the believers in the relic say, a blood-stained image of the face of Christ. Is there any interesting causal connection between the Sudarium and the face of Christ that is also found between a mirror image and its original? Or is it just that thanks to some causal connection or other, an image is produced that we *see as* the face of Christ, given how we now imagine that face?

Let us ring the changes on causation just a little longer. Consider then the strange case of the Shroud of Turin, where some have alleged that a *supernatural* causality, having to do with Christ's resurrected body emanating though the Shroud, was behind the truly incredible image on that famous piece of linen. Suppose for a moment that those supporters of the relic had been right in this; then it would also be right to say that the image on the Shroud is the image *of* the crucified body of Christ. But how can this pattern of supernatural causation also be assimilated to the paradigm pattern supposedly required for a natural representation to be *of* or *about* its original? Or is it just that, however the Shroud was produced, we have there an image that *puts us in mind of* the crucified Christ (as we now imagine him)?

If that is right, it simply a mistake to think that there is a characteristic pattern of causation that is required for a natural representation to be *of* or *about* a certain original item. The role of causation here is just to create something that has certain features that enable us to use it to bring to mind the original. And that may mean, as it does in the case of the crucified Christ, just *imagining* the original.

Turn now to the issue of resemblance. A story is told of Igor Stravinsky, who was getting increasingly irritated by a talkative man in the train seat alongside him. When the man, after describing his young wife in glowing terms, reached into his pocket and pulled out a wallet-sized photograph of her, Stravinsky cupped the photo in both hands and then remarked, "She is quite small, isn't she?" Had Stravinsky been even more irritated, he might have asked, "What must it be like living with such a two-dimensional person?"

In looking at photographs, and seeing them as representations of their originals, we have learned to ignore the manifest dissimilarities between image and original. Likewise, the images on the walls of *camerae obscurae*, and in mirrors, are in many ways nothing like their originals. We have learned to construe such images, that is, to focus on similarities between image and original, and to neglect "irrelevant" differences.

By considerations like these we can be led to realize that the paradigm cases of natural representation were just cases in which we found it natural to use the image to put us in mind of the original. They were not instances of a natural two-place relation of intentionality or *aboutness* holding between image and original, instances that we then could explore in order to find the favorable mix of causation and resemblance that makes a representation *about* its original. Rather they were instances of the three-place relation of *our* finding it natural to use the *image* to put us in mind of *the original*. In this relation our intentional attitude directed to the image is crucial, and in a way that bodes ill for any reductive account of intentionality that relies on "natural representation" as its inspiration.

Representation and "Carrying Information"

Still, many philosophers just cannot see how we could be anything other than Producers of Presence, and so they still maintain faith in there being some kind of correct Representationalist treatment of mental states.

So, it is said, representational states "carry" descriptive information thanks to their history and intrinsic characteristics. The standard analogy is with the rings in a tree trunk, which carry information about just how old the tree is. Here, too, however, we seem to be suppressing something important about the real relation in play. The rings in the tree trunk carry information about the age of the tree *relative to certain techniques of examination and interpretation.*

Still, let us allow that something can be made of certain brain states carrying descriptive information. The Representionalist idea may now be put like this: those states are *of* or *about* some item in the external environment just in case that item is the unique satisfier of that descriptive information.

It fills one with an uncanny sense of déjà vu. For it a parallels a well-known thesis about the reference of names, one discussed earlier, according to which a name gets to refer to a unique individual because that individual uniquely satisfies the descriptive information somehow associated with the name. So if Plato is the greatest philosopher of antiquity, then by associating the description "the greatest philosopher of antiquity" with the name "Plato," one can use that name to refer to Plato.

But as we have already seen, this quite natural and appealing thesis was decisively refuted by Saul Kripke in his lectures *Naming and Necessity*. Kripke's observations were as follows. First, for many names that refer, there is no uniquely identifying descriptive content known to the user of the name. Second, it is often the case that the associated descriptive content happens to be false of the bearer of the name. Third, even when the associated descriptive content is true of the bearer of the name, it is often only contingently true of the bearer of the name, and so cannot be the basis of our referring to the bearer of the name in possible situations in which the descriptive content does not hold true of the bearer of the name. So we can entertain the true thought that Plato might not have pursued philosophy. Therefore it cannot be that the content of the name "Plato" as it appears in that thought is given by the description "the greatest philosopher of antiquity" (*modulo* considerations of the scope of the description). For in the envisaged possibility the description would pick out Aristotle, and not Plato.

These arguments against the usefulness of descriptive content in determining the reference of conventional representations like names can be adapted to apply to the thesis that a natural representation, understood as carrying descriptive content, is about the item in the world that satisfies the descriptive content. The descriptive content may be false of the item represented, it may fall far short of distinguishing the item represented from similar items, and the representation may continue to represent the item even in circumstances in which the item is counterfactually supposed not to satisfy the descriptive content. We shall, however, have to wait a little while to see just *why* these adaptations of Kripke's arguments work.

Kripke's arguments against the usefulness of descriptive content in determining the reference of names pushed several philosophers back to the claim that the crucial condition for a name's being about a given individual was the holding of the right causal connection between the utterance of a name on a given occasion and some original baptism in which the name was attached to the bearer. In effect, they took this to be the lesson of *Naming and Necessity.*[5] But this looks like a confusion between the linguistic genealogy of the use of a name, and something that could ground reference to an item.

Causation is in itself too promiscuous a relation to make for any natural connection between a present use of a specific name and an original "baptism" of some item with that name. Consider two uses of the name "Gavrilo Princip": the one by his mother in response to the question "What is your son's name?" thereby identifying him to the Bosnian police who were seeking the assassin of Archduke Franz Ferdinand, and the other by a contemporary high school student who has gleaned the name from the Internet, and first misspelled it badly, only then to fall into the correct spelling, and so write the name "Gavrilo Princip." Are we seriously to suppose that there is some common causal connection that holds between each of the two uses or *tokenings* of the name "Gavrilo Princip" and the event of the naming of the man Gavrilo Princip, a connection whose holding *makes it the case* that each tokening of the name refers to the man?

As Kripke himself observed, there may be a chain of mental acts, *each with its own unreduced intentional content*, leading back to the relevant original naming or "baptism," so that with every new use of the name, the speaker at least intends to refer to the same person as was referred to by those from which he first learned the name. (Maybe; but Gavrilo's mother would be rather strange if she had *that* intention. She presumably simply intended to refer to her son.) Even so, there is no reason to think that underlying such chains of referential intentions there is any interesting or distinctive causal pattern that would itself *ground* reference.

5. See, in particular, Dennis Stamp, "Towards a Causal Theory of Linguistic Representation," *Midwest Studies in Philosophy* 2 (1977); Hartry Field, "Mental Representation," *Erekentnis* 13 (1978); Michael Devitt, *Designation* (Cambridge University Press, 1981); and Fred Dretske, *Knowledge and the Flow of Information* (MIT Press, 1981).

CAN CAUSATION ACCOUNT FOR ABOUTNESS?

Well, if it is not satisfaction of descriptive content that makes for the crucial connection between a representation and what it represents, then what could it possibly be, if not some relevant pattern of causal connection there in the world?

"Some relevant pattern of causal connection" is a mantra of misbegotten hopefulness, and for two reasons. First, suppose that sometime in the next decade, we actually found it. It would be a highly abstract pattern that could hold not only between thoughts supposedly involving a mental representation of Plato and the philosopher Plato, but also between thoughts supposedly involving a mental representation of Gavrilo Princip and the assassin Gavrilo Princip. Now consider some variant on that pattern, and ask: What is it about the first causal pattern, and not its variant, that, as it were, makes the lights of intentionality go on—that is, makes it the case that certain inner states of individuals are intentionally directed toward items in the environment? How does figuring at different ends of one kind of complex causal web make for intentionality, while similarly figuring in different but equally complex causal webs leaves the world devoid of intentionality? That is a pressing question because what is on offer is supposed to be *a reduction* of intentionality, and such a reduction ought to make it clear why such a phenomenon, which has a certain natural unity, should depend for its existence on this or that tweaking of detailed causal connections.

Second, the very idea of causation breaks into three parts. Consider the event that is the tokening in some brain of some putative representation. There is, first of all, the notion of the total cause of that event. The total cause of any given event is an objective feature of the event, and could be identified with the whole event structure in the past light cone of the given event. Then there is the notion of what might be called the in-itself-sufficient producer of the event, that is, the subpart of the past light cone which is such that if it were duplicated, then an event of exactly the same sort would be produced. Then there is the notion of *a notable cause* of the event, a notion on which my neglecting my plants caused their withering, while Queen Elizabeth's neglecting them did not. This is a notion inherently connected with our interest in practices of explaining, predicting, duplicating, and preventing events—practices that lead us to focus on small parts of the event structure in the past light cone, parts which are salient to us, and which are of a kind with events we might imagine manipulating to produce, or prevent, similar effects in the future. Accordingly, the notion of a notable cause is an anthropocentric notion in the way that the notions of the total cause or the sufficient producer of an event are not.

Return now to the respective thoughts about Gavrilo Princip had by his mother and by the high school student who came across him on the Internet. Gavrilo does not exhaust the past light cones of those thoughts. He is not an in-itself-sufficient producer of those thoughts. At most, Gavrilo figures as a notable (albeit in the one case very remote) cause of each thought. This suggests that in the proposed reductive accounts of intentionality by way of causation, the ordinary notion of a notable cause must be invoked. But it seems paradoxical that a rather gerrymandered relation of being a notable cause, a relation that is salient to us only because of our practices of explanation, prediction, and prevention, should be the crucial relation to be appealed to in the reduction of intentionality. Intentionality, and this is particularly obvious when it comes to perceptual intentionality, is a phenomenon with a certain natural unity; we do not seem to be properly explicating that unity by appealing to an anthropocentric notion like being a notable cause.[6] Intentionality is a relation whose adequate demarcation is *less* anthropocentric than that of being a notable cause. It would, then, be very surprising if intentionality can be reduced to the relation of notable causation plus whatever else.

It should go without saying that this is not in any way to deny that we are often caused by external objects to go into intentional states directed toward them. That is a manifest fact, which in no way implies that intentionality can be *reduced to* causation plus something else.

It is worth recalling a final embarrassment for the thesis that it is by way of a distinguished pattern of causation that representations get to

6. A point also made by Hilary Putnam. See his important work *Representation and Reality* (Bradford Books, 1991) for a similarly skeptical treatment of the very idea of natural representation.

be about what they are about. We often think about abstract entities, items not located in the causal network, items that are not causes of anything; either our thinking of them is not representing them to ourselves, or causation is not a necessary condition for representation.

What Could Replace the Representationalist Tradition?

A short summary of the last forty years of work on the attempt to reduce intentionality might be put this way. If we take *aboutness* to be a relation holding contingently between a (re)presentation and an item it is supposedly about, then we do not find any good account of what that relation is. It is not the relation of satisfying an individuating descriptive content, and it is not any of the three canvassed relations of causation. And the favorable mix of description and causation seems to have eluded us. That is where we now are in the so-called metaphysics of content.

In a way, we should have suspected this all along, particularly if we had taken to heart the idea that the connection between a state that makes something present and what it makes present is not an accidental feature of that state but enters into the essence of that state, partly defining what it is to be that state.

Of course, even with all that said, there is nothing wrong with using the idiom or analogy of representation in an empirical subpersonal psychology, say in order to mark steps of information processing in the brain and nervous system.[7] In such a subpersonal psychology, "representing that P" means carrying the information or the misinformation that P. This is the sense in which the rings in a tree trunk might represent the age of the tree. They are traces from which the age of the tree can be recovered. And perhaps, as the work of Ruth Millikan and others

---

7. Several theorists have been careful to make the distinction between a naturalistic reduction of intentionality by way of "representations" and the status of the idea of representational content in cognitive science. See Robert Cummings, *Meaning and Mental Representation* (MIT Press, 1989); Stephen Stitch, "What Is a Theory of Mental Representation?" *Mind* 101 (1992); and Michael Tye, "Naturalism and the Mental," *Mind* 101 (1992).

suggests,[8] in explicating this relation of carrying information, we may find it helpful to resort to the idea of evolved proper functioning in order to allow that a tree that does not grow *properly* can leave misleading traces as to its age, so that its rings can carry *misinformation* about its age.

That is perfectly all right as it stands; but the thing to see is how little this sort of representation (namely, bearing a trace from which information or misinformation can be recovered) is like the *presentational* nature of our mental states.

Recall the earlier remarks about perception. When one sees one's dogs running in the front yard, one is not simply getting into an information-bearing state from which it is possible to recover the fact that one's dogs are running in the front yard. Instead, the whole content of the perceptual experience is of the dogs and their running being present to oneself, of being available in a certain way. In being thus available, the dogs are "closer" than any mere cause of one's inner information-bearing states could be. THERE they are, immediately available as objects of demonstration, and as topics of one's further thought and talk. What does the philosophy of mental representation make of this immediate *availability*, the flood of new topics of thought and talk that comes upon us every time we open our ears and eyes?

I recall driving along a road through the forest on the way to Yosemite; on the car stereo Glenn Gould was mangling the French Suites in his typically riveting way. During the long trip, I saw thousands of trees and heard thousands of notes. They flashed by, yet each was presented to me as distinct from the others. The whole phenomenology of the experience had a certain "donatory" aspect, in that the individual trees and the notes were just given to me without any attentive effort on my part.

There is no doubt that this was because of the operation of my visual and auditory system. But there are two ways of understanding this undeniable fact. On the first, thanks to that neural operation (which, by the way, we might well describe and *model* in information-processing

---

8. See Ruth Millikan, *Language, Thought, and Other Biological Categories* (MIT Press, 1984) and "In Defense of Proper Functions," *Philosophy of Science* 56 (1989).

terms), the trees and the notes became present—that is, a host of modes of presentation of the trees and the notes were accessed, and thus made up the content of my conscious life during the trip. That is why each tree and note was available to me as a potential object of attention, demonstration, and thought.

There is a second, Representationalist, way of understanding the undeniable fact that the trees and the notes were made available by the operation of my visual and auditory systems. The Representationalist would say that the trees and the notes were made available to me at the level of conscious awareness because a host of individual representations of those trees and notes were *produced* in my sensory system. For each tree and each note, my sensory representational system had already formed some representational designatum that then made the tree or the note *available* in this way.

Now the crucial question: How does such an appeal to representations in any way *explain* the availability of the tree and the notes? The Representationalist analogies with rings in a tree or with beavers signaling with their tails involve nothing like availability. Availability simply does not figure in the Representationalist Theory of Mind—unless, that is, we help ourselves to the "homuncularist" dead end encouraged by the *camera obscura*, the idea of perception as involving a subject contemplating his own representations. This is obviously a dead end because it rests everything on the *availability to a subject of his own representations*, a primary intentional attitude of just the sort that the Representationalist is trying to reduce. And now, once again, whatever favorable mix of description, causation, and proper function we invoke, the availability of the representation, and thus of the items it represents, will not be accounted for.

This shows that when it comes to availability, the resort to representations does no work; either we can say that thanks to the operation of our sensory systems items in the environment are made available, or we can say that thanks to the operation of our sensory systems there come to be representations that make items in the environment available. The first is a fact, and the second is a pseudoexplanation, for the idiom of representation does not in any way illuminate perceptual availability, the way in which the objects of perception are

THERE, and so able to be demonstrated and taken as new topics of thought and talk.

A Diagnosis of the Representationalist's Mistake

That point about perception, the way it makes its objects available for demonstration, thought, and talk, along with the failure over the past forty years to find the favorable mix of description, causation, and proper function that makes for *aboutness*, might prompt us to take a different tack. The problematic assumption in the philosophical treatment of intentionality is that the basic form of intentionality has the structure of a mental (or brain) representation being *contingently related*, be it by causation or individuating description or whatever, to an item represented. Since it is of the nature of mental (or brain) representations to contingently relate to items in the environment, we need to find some non-Representationalist way of conceiving of intentionality.

In order to take a different tack, we might begin by adapting Gottlob Frege's terminology, and speak of "senses" or "modes of presentation" making up our mental acts of experiencing, believing, and thinking.[9] We should not think of these acts as the generation of representations that somehow carry or encode modes of presentation; instead we are to think of their whole intellectual and sensory content as given by the constitutive modes in which their targets or topics present.

Next, we are to think of these modes of presentation as objective (if sometimes relational) features of the things themselves. This is the idea that each item that could be a topic of thought and talk has associated with it a host of standing ways, or manners, or modes, of presenting.

A so-called subjective mental act is, then, to be thought of as an act of accessing a mode of presentation of the items that the act thereby is about. The whole experienced character of the mental act is determined by that accessed mode of presentation, not by the character of some experienced representation.

9. See "The Thought," in *The Frege Reader*, ed. Michael Beaney (Blackwell, 1997).

Finally, and crucially, we must drop Frege's (somewhat throwaway) suggestion that we understand modes of presentation as something like individuating descriptions: things that need not be essentially related to the items they do in fact pick out. Instead, we should understand a mode of presentation of an item as individuated partly by the item presented! So, for example, a mode of presentation of the dog Jasper is *Jasper*-presenting-in-a-certain-way.

Given that, we can see why counterparts of Kripke's results in *Naming and Necessity* hold against the view that individuating descriptive content determines what a natural representation is about. Those results and their counterparts are exactly what one should expect if modes of presentation are partly individuated by what they present. So conceived, modes of presentation might well not carry uniquely identifying descriptive material about the items they present. Indeed, they may even be false of the items they present, as in the case of illusion.

Even in the case of illusion, the object of the illusion is *presented* by way of an illusory mode of presentation. That is why one can come to secure one's first demonstrative reference to an item on the basis of an illusory presentation of the item. As when, on a hike through the hills, your friend points to a dot on a far hillside, something that turns out to be a camper's hut. Seeing the dot, you can ask, "Is *that* the hut we have been looking for?" The hut is presented, despite the fact that it is not a dot, that is, despite the descriptive falsity or illusory character of the presentation. The whole content of the illusory experience is the hut presenting as "a dot" on the distant hillside. Because it is the hut presenting in that way, the hut is THERE, available for demonstration, thought, and talk.

Here, then, is the parting of the ways with Frege, who otherwise is our model for thinking of objective modes of presentation. It is misleading to say, as Frege does, that a mode of presentation *determines* a referent; a mode of presentation *is just* a referent, some item or other in the world, presenting in a certain manner. The mode or manner of presentation no more determines a referent than your last flu inoculation determines you. Just as that inoculation was partly individuated in terms of its being *yours*, a mode of presentation is partly individuated in terms of the very item it presents.

Consider, by analogy, an object that can be picked up only in certain ways by beings with hands like ours. The object, because of its shape and size, itself determines a number of adequate manners of lifting it. For example, if it is a large log, then, because of its size and shape, one manner of lifting it will be by using two arms cupped underneath at a sufficient distance to balance the log. These manners of lifting the log can certainly be generalized, and applied to other logs of similar sorts, but in the first instance they are simply further relational features of the very log in question. As well as the log's size and shape, there are just *these* ways of lifting the log. Other ways of engaging with the log are just not *ways of lifting the log.* There is no sensible question as to what further relation is such that its holding between the log and a certain manner of lifting makes that manner of lifting a manner of lifting *that very log.*

The manners and the log are not related merely accidentally; the log partly individuates any manner of lifting *it.* Notice, by the way, how odd it would be to explain the relation between the log and manners of lifting it by appealing to intermediate representations that are somehow *about* the log. But again, this is not to preempt the question of whether in the empirical psychology of action it is useful to model our motor system as an information-processing system. The way to apply such a model would then be as an account of how we are able to do such things as lift logs—that is, *implement* certain ways of lifting logs.

From this point of view, the tradition went wrong in treating modes of presentation as not essentially related to what they make present, so that there was then a gap to be filled, either by description or by causation, a gap between some mental representation and the worldly items which that mental item makes present. But modes of presentation are not mental; they are objective, in that they come with the objects themselves as the very features of those objects that make them available for demonstration, thought, and talk. And they are individuated by the objects they present along with the manners in which they present those objects.

Among the objects that come with their respective modes of presentation are abstract objects; so there is no *special* problem produced by reference to abstract objects, as there was in the Representationalist tradition.

It should be added that none of this is at odds with the causal completeness of brain science, taken on its own terms. As a result of my brain going into a certain state, I access a particular mode of presentation of a particular item. That is how I come to think about the item. This is no less empirical or naturalistic than the alternative explanation, which has it that as a result of my brain's going into a certain state, I enjoy a representation whose content is that a certain item is a certain way. *These are two theories that are equally compatible with the very same patterns of causation in the brain and the sensory systems.* It just that the second account has extra empirical claims not made by the first, claims about the existence of representations that carry or express contents or manners of presentation. Those extra claims will be idle empirical claims, unless they play some distinctive explanatory role. And the distinctive role they were meant to play, namely, providing for a reductive account of intentionality, is not a viable role. Therefore mental representations are fifth wheels.[10]

A Transformed Picture of "Consciousness" and Reality

Our occurrent mental acts, our experiences and our thoughts, are occasions of accessing objective modes of presentation of items. So our mental lives are filled with objective features of external items, namely, their modes of presentation. But we get nowhere near exhausting the modes of presentation that there are. For example, there is a way things look to a being like you from three feet northeast from here now, even if no one is ever occupying that perceptual standpoint. You could have accessed that way things look if you had occupied that position; but your accessing this objective, if relational, mode of presentation would make no difference to its character or to what it presents.

The transformed picture of reality associated with this idea can be brought out very simply. When you close your eyes, the objects before you are still looking the way they just did; more generally, without you

---

10. At this juncture, the reader may well be wondering how the antirepresentational account could possibly handle hallucination and afterimaging, where nothing real is presenting to the subject of the experience. For a suggestion as to how to handle such cases, see "The Obscure Object of Hallucination."

on the scene they would still present in the whole variety of ways in which they now present to you. They would just not be available to you. Furthermore, if that is not eerie enough, given that there are animals or conscious minds with sensibilities unlike ours, the objects before you now present in a host of ways that you could never access. (For we should think of these other animals as also sampling presence, in their respective idiosyncratic ways.) The specificity of your sensibility, the detailed structure of your sensory and cognitive apparatus, in effect blinkers you to all but a very narrow range of modes of presentation of the items before you. You do not produce presence; you only selectively access it in your mental acts. What you call the contents of your mind are out there already.

Presence is therefore not a subjective phenomenon. As we shall see, properly understood, there are no subjective phenomena. There is a host of events that fill our so-called subjective mental lives. These events are occurrent mental acts, which are objective psychological occurrences. Their contents are objective modes of presentation. These modes of presentation are standing properties of the objects themselves. It is because they have these standing properties, anyway, that the objects themselves are intelligible to the intellect, and available to be sensed in a variety of ways.

On this view our respective mental lives are just particular idiosyncratic histories of *accessing* objective modes of presentation. What we accessed were objects presenting in this or that way; our metal lives are parasitic on this ubiquitous fact of presentation. We are not Producers of Presence; that is, we are not beings whose psychological operations are the preconditions of presence. The whole content of our minds is the contribution of the objects. When we speak of consciousness, we are systematically getting hold of the wrong end of the stick; the basic reality is not the fact of consciousness, understood as the inner achievement of a mind. It is the fact of the continuous and multifaceted disclosure of objects, which certain evolved animals are able to access.

CONFIRMING THE SURPRISING HYPOTHESIS

Even without our minds, the objects would still be presenting in all the ways they do. (The world would be devoid only of our metal acts, and of the modes of presentation that would present those acts in further acts of reflective consciousness.) To be sure, given our Representationalist weltanschauung the idea of presence without anyone accessing presence is so surprising as to be almost unintelligible; for we are like the members of a borrowing library who narcissistically suppose that their acts of borrowing *create* the books they borrow. We take ourselves to be Producers of Presence; that is, we take presence to be dependent on our mental operations.

Here is a way of providing empirical confirmation of the hypothesis that presence is not mind-dependent. Stare at something in your immediate field of vision. Attend to how that thing looks. Now, without moving your head in any direction, just close your eyes, and consider the hypothesis that it still looks THAT way, the very way it looked when you had your eyes open. You can confirm this hypothesis by *now opening your eyes.* Associated with this confirmation may be a certain metaphysical gestalt shift in which we experience our minds as "out there already."

Of course, those philosophers who suppose that a thing's looking a certain way is nothing other than our enjoying a representation of it, will treat our little performance as an example of the "refrigerator light" fallacy. You open the refrigerator door; the light is on. You close it and hypothesize that the light is still on when the refrigerator door is closed. You then confirm that the light is still on by opening the door again. In this case, they will say, you have confirmed no such thing, for there is a mechanism built in to the refrigerator that turns off the light when the door is closed.

But actually, upon reflection, it is hard to see why there need be any *fallacy* in the refrigerator light inference. (It is an inductive inference, and not every inductive inference with a true premise and a false conclusion is an inductive fallacy.) Suppose there were no such special mechanism that turns off the light when the refrigerator door is closed, and turns it on when it is open: then surely my opening the door and closing it, and opening it again and seeing the light again, would be good evidence that the light is continuously on. It would be just like checking twice to see that paint on your car is dry. This is a way of confirming the hypothesis that the paint is dry, dry anyway, that is, even when no one is checking. The difference in the refrigerator light case is just that, as things stand now, our total evidence about actual refrigerators ought to include knowledge of a special mechanism that turns the light off and on.

Compare the situation with our little performance. Those philosophers who believe that an object's looking a certain way is nothing other than our enjoying a mental representation of that object, are thereby proposing a mechanism that, as it were, turns the mental lights off and on. When you were staring at the object before you, it was present because you were enjoying a mental representation of it. When you closed your eyes, it was not present because you were not enjoying a mental representation of it. When you opened your eyes, it became present again because once again you were enjoying a mental representation of it. Given the mechanism, the inference we made in our little performance was just like the naive inference that the refrigerator light is continuously on.

The only problem is that we have quite good reasons to believe that the proposed mechanism is *not* operating. Those reasons are the very ones we were illustrating by quickly rehearsing the failure of forty years of dedicated philosophical work, the failure to give anything like a satisfactory account of how a mental representation could be *of* or *about* anything in the external world, at least in the way that a perception of something is *of* or *about* that thing, a way that makes what it is about available for further demonstration, thought, and talk. Having a mental representation caused by an object that the representation "resembles" is nothing like having that object present in the way that objects present in perceptual experience. As for causation, similarity, and proper function, there seems to be no favorable mix of these external relations that would make objects available in the way they are in perception.

In the absence of this proposed mechanism of representation, our little performance should be understood as more like checking twice to see that the paint job on one's car has dried. This performance provides very good evidence that the painted surface of the car continues to have the relevant property of being dry *unperceived*, and so even when it is not being touched. So also, our little performance provides very good evidence of the continued presence, *unperceived*, of the object to which you were attending. That is, it looks the way it does even when you are not accessing that way it looks. Try it a few times, and see if you can't get the feeling that the contents of your mind are "out there already."

So here, again, is the neglected hypothesis, hopefully by now more vividly in view. We are not Producers of Presence; it is not that our mental acts make things present. We are Samplers of Presence; our mental acts are samplings from a vast realm of objective manners of presentation. It is of the nature of existents to present, in all the various ways in which they can be grasped in this or that mental act of this or that individual mind. The modes of presentation are all there on the side of the things themselves. Those modes of presentation are just the things presenting in this or that way. They provide the whole content of our mental acts.

Of course, some of these mental acts, in their turn, are presented only to me, and some are presented only to you. So we have my thoughts and experiences, and your thoughts and experiences. But properly understood, this is not a subjective phenomenon either. I see my dogs running in the front yard. Here I access modes of presentation of my dogs. Those modes of presentation are as objective as the dogs themselves. (You could have accessed the same or similar modes of presentation of my dogs running, if you had been situated in my viewing position.) Now consider the mental act of my seeing my dogs running in the front yard, something present to me and not to you. Only I am in a position to have reflective awareness of this act, and to remember it later on. But this looks like a contingent fact, no doubt a rock-solid one, having something to do with the causal isolation of our respective brain processes.

There is nothing subjective, or mind-dependent, about presence. If that is so, then there is no danger that death, even the death of the last conscious being, will secure the end of presence. At most, the danger is that certain evolved animals will cease to access presence. Things will cease to be available to them. But how things appear, how they present—all this would remain completely the same, down to the last detail.

Chapter 10

The Mind of God

The Objectivity of the Realm of Sense

We are not Producers of Presence; it is not that our mental acts make things present. We are Samplers of Presence; our mental acts are samplings from a vast realm of objective manners of presentation. It is of the nature of existents to present, in all the various ways in which they can be grasped in this or that mental act of this or that individual mind. The manners of presentation are all there on the side of the things themselves. Those manners of presentation are just the things presenting in this or that way.

All the manners of presentation or disclosure of things, all the ways of thinking of them, and experiencing them, come with the things themselves. What we call an individual consciousness is no more than a particular history of sampling from this vast realm, a history of accessing manners of presentation.

How the Structure of Presence Might Impose Evolutionary Constraints

Given our hypothesis, it is natural to go on to suppose that the vast totality of modes of presentation has some significant structure, and may indeed exhibit a *limited variety* of types of modes of presentation. This would set an antecedent limit on the types of evolvable systems of cognition, memory, and perception. There are only certain directions in which biological systems can evolve in order to be able to access one or another of the limited variety of types of modes of presentation, and so take advantage of one or another form of consciousness.

.

In this way, an independent structure of the objective realm of presence or disclosure could itself impose constraints on what would be a viable form of conscious bodily life.

For example, consider the modes of presentation of ostensible features of the surfaces of things, in particular of those qualities that are the colors. We know that birds have a much more sophisticated visual system than we do, at least in the sense of having a fourth set of cones compared to our three, so that the phenomenology of their color experience must be very different from ours. So we might be led to speak of the birds' colors and our colors, and think of surfaces as objectively presenting in both ways.

However, since attention to a range of qualities like the colors presented by objects is among the most salient ways of making out distinctions among objects, and of tracing them, and of detecting the chemical differences that in part map the difference between the edible and the inedible, we can think of both humans and birds in the evolutionary development of their visual systems as having been under a general and quite objective constraint, in effect a selective pressure, imposed as it were from the side of the realm of sense. Expressed as a command, this selective pressure would come to this: other things being equal, develop neurally in such a way that you can access a range of colorlike qualitative manners of presentation of objects, so as to be better able to distinguish objects, trace them, and make out useful differences like friend and foe, and edible and inedible.

In this way, the antecedent objective structure of modes of presentation can impose a variety of fates, promising and unpromising, on any developing form of conscious life. If that is so, then the selective environment in which evolution operates has been massively and systematically underdescribed; it is not just the physical structure of the environment, but it is the antecedent structure of the limited variety of modes of presentation that can in principle be accessed by the variety of neural systems that might get going in that environment.

This point, that selective pressures are imposed not just by the physical environment, but by the antecedent structure of modes of presentation of the items that make up the environment, applies a fortiori to the development of intellectual life. There may be a limited variety of ways of thinking about things, so that an animal that begins to develop rudimentary thought, and thereby derives some selective advantage, may have had to develop physically in such a way as to be able to access one or another of these ways of thinking about things. In this way, the antecedent structure of the realm of presence can partly impose a variety of fates, promising and unpromising, on any developing form of intellectual life.

In this way, Objective Mind—the totality of objective modes of presentation—could play an explanatory role. It could set limits on which forms of individual mental life will be viable. So it is at least in principle possible, compatible with the causal completeness of the physical description of every transaction in the world, that what takes place in the development of the neural basis of mind is partly ordained by the independent structure of presence, that is, by Objective Mind.[1]

One homely version of this suggestion might already be accepted by those mathematical realists who suppose that the numbers constitute an objective realm, with its own structure there to be grasped. It need not be supposed that the numbers themselves could have any causal efficacy; still, the objective structure of mathematical reality will impose a variety of fates, promising and unpromising, on any living thing that is becoming numerate. You either correctly map parts of this realm in your thought, or your incipient attempts at quantitative reasoning will make grave trouble for you. That "demand" presumably has been a selective pressure in our actual evolutionary development. To say something like this is not at all to dabble in the shallow and murky waters of intelligent design.

But now simply generalize from the antecedent structure of mathematical reality to the antecedent structure of presence. This structure, too, may impose its selective pressures. And in this way, Objective Mind may determine what forms of mental life are viable, and may do this without exercising any causal influence on material processes.

---

1. The relevant notion of explanation would be a development of the idea of a "program explanation," an idea developed by Frank Jackson and Philip Pettit; see, for example, their "Program Explanation: A General Perspective," *Analysis* 50 (1990).

Objective Mind and the Mind of the Highest One

In Objective Mind—the objective structure of modes of presentation that make up the realm of sense—there are hosts of illusory, inadequate, and incomplete modes of presentation. It presumably must be so, since evolution consists in gradual adaptation, and the ability to access some primitive modes of thinking of things, and correspondingly limited modes of experiencing things, will still confer a selective advantage on animals even though those modes of presentation are far from fully accurate presentations. Still, there does seem to be some competitive advantage conferred by shedding illusion and clarifying our thoughts into an increasingly integrated explanatory structure. The resulting, more accurate forms of understanding will exploit more and more adequate and complete modes of presentation.

At the idealized limit of this process of deepening understanding, we would come to grasp those modes of presentation of reality that are fully adequate and complete, and so reveal the nature of what they present. In this sense, we would be conforming our minds to the Divine Mind, which may be construed as the totality of fully adequate and complete modes of presentation of reality.

Of course, this is an ideal limit, and who can tell what transformations of individual minds and bodily structures would be required to better approximate to it. Nevertheless, part of the self-disclosure of the Highest One involves the disclosure of his mind, by way of our movement in the direction of deepening understanding.

A comparison with the evolutionary significance of increasing cooperation may be helpful here. It is not that the normative principles of cooperation and kin altruism could have any *causal* influence on evolution and natural selection. It is just that, as a matter of fact, animals that are prepared to cooperate with their kin, and to some extent sacrifice their interests for those kin, confer a collective advantage on their kin and clan. To that extent, cooperative and kin-altruistic animals are likely to become more numerous in evolutionary history. The same holds for animals with mental capacities that enable them to grasp more adequate and complete modes of presentation.

Here, then, is a variant on Hegel's theme of the cunning of history; you might call it the cunning of nature. There is a natural selective pressure to develop more adequate ideas, to deepen understanding, and this takes us in the direction of gradually conforming our minds to the Mind of God, understood as the totality of fully adequate modes of presentation.

THE DOUBLY DONATORY CHARACTER OF REALITY

The distinction between the realm of sense and the realm of nature may give the wrong impression. In reality there are not two separate realms; there is Being-making-itself-present-to-beings. If we take presence for granted and set about investigating the causes of things, then a certain grand object of investigation will come into view, a domain that deserves the name of the realm of nature. We should remember that we did take presence for granted in all this, and that our success in describing the causal lineaments of the realm of nature does not indicate that presence itself is some sort of causal transaction, ultimately reducible to mass-energy transfer or something like that.

Reality is Being-making-itself-present-to-beings, not a sort of conjunction or fusion of two realms, the realm of sense and the realm of nature. Given the earlier insight gleaned from our Platonic reading of Thomas, we can open up this general form of reality a little more. The beings, that is, each and every creaturely thing that exists, are themselves exemplifications of Being. Each is, as it were, precipitated or individuated out of Being, and is thus none other than a finite expression of Being, distinctive thanks to its distinctive finite essence or principle of individuation.

So the general form of reality is at least the outpouring of Being itself by way of its exemplification in ordinary beings and its self-disclosure to some of those beings.

Seeing reality in that way, holding that frame in place as the basic frame in which one experiences the world, supports a profound background feeling of gratitude in response to the "doubly donatory" character of reality. First, I am an expression of Being Itself, as are all the things present to me, as Dylan Thomas puts it: "the force that through the green fuse drives the flower drives my green life." Second, all of THIS is made available to me, gratis. Whatever happens then, I have already been endowed with great gifts; I have already won the cosmic lottery. Seeing all this, perhaps I can then begin to overcome the centripetal force of the self, the condition of being *incurvatus in se*, and instead turn toward reality and the real needs of others.

Does this not resemble in some ways—of course it is transposed into a quite different key—what Spinoza means when he refers to "the intellectual love of God"? And perhaps, as Spinoza himself thought, once we open up in this way, there is even a further grace to be received from the idea of Christ, something that we will explore below.

Does God Exist?

Still, the great religions of God, Judaism, Christianity, and Islam, want something *more* than this, something more than the doubly donatory character of reality. They are religions of salvation history, of a God in search of us for the sake of our salvation. The only God they will recognize is a God in search of us—to be sure, a God thereby shown to be probably mad, but leave that alone. And this, that God is in search of us, is a further incredible proposition. Especially so, now that we know how utterly insignificant the earth, the home of humanity, actually is from the naturalistic point of view. In our terms, the monotheisms want to say something like this:

> The outpouring of Being by way of its exemplification in ordinary existents *is for the sake of* the self-disclosure of Being *to us*.

The replacement of a conjunction by a loaded connective, and the addition of an absolutely special place for us: the truth of monotheism turns on this? Yes. But look at the earth, and look at the vast immensity of space and time . . . How *could* this claim of monotheism be true?

Suppose, then, that something less than this were true; suppose it were the case that

> The outpouring of Being by way of its exemplification in ordinary existents *is for the sake of* the self-disclosure of Being.

Then, even though monotheism would be false, a panentheist would say that God exists. For God would just be the outpouring of Being by way of its exemplification in ordinary existents for the sake of the self-disclosure of Being.

If what was said above about the cunning of nature is true, this "for the sake of" is not an idea flatly inconsistent with legitimate naturalism.

Now suppose, finally, that the introduction of the teleological idiom *is still* misplaced. Even so, we would have the doubly donatory character of reality, and lived attention to that might be enough to overcome the centripetal force of self-love.

The Highest One

Our method was to bracket questions of existence, in order to understand what God would be if there were a God. Once the familiar conceptions of God are purged of their idolatrous elements, once we see that a true conception of God must be fully compatible with the completeness of natural science in its own domain, we arrive at this account of the Highest One:

> The Highest One = the outpouring of Being by way of its exemplification in ordinary existents for the sake of the self-disclosure of Being.

We also adapted from the tradition of the three monotheisms a vivid sense that our thought and talk developed as tools for engaging with ordinary existents, so that we are forced to draw on analogy in thinking and speaking of the Highest One. Accordingly, the Love of the Highest One was analogized as its outpouring in ordinary existents, its Will as self-disclosure, its Mind as the most revealing presentations found in the realm of sense, and its Power as the totality of the laws of nature. In these respects, the Highest One has by analogy the characteristics of a person, but a person far removed from ordinary personality.

Again, it can hardly be overemphasized, these are, of necessity, analogical ways of thinking of the Highest One, chosen here because they explicitly discourage the idolatrous hope for a Cosmic Intervener who might confer special worldly advantages on his favorites. The Great Advantage, the outpouring and self-disclosure that is the Highest One, has already been conferred.

There will be general skepticism as to whether any such religious outlook could matter to "ordinary people of faith." Yet perhaps it is already incipient in their faith. They pray, and their prayers are not in fact answered, at least not by way of any intervention by a god. But, even so, they keep their faith in life, and in the importance of goodness. In this they are like Job, and they recapitulate in their lives the meaning of the book of Job.

The meaning of the book of Job is not that we should keep our mouths shut in the face of divine majesty and power; the meaning is the moral and religious irrelevance of Yahweh and all the putative Cosmic Interveners. Recall how it goes: Yahweh is challenged to a wager by the Satan, who bets that Job is faithful to Yahweh only because his worldly life has gone exceedingly well. So Yahweh lets the Satan destroy Job's life step-by-step, to see if he will remain faithful. Job perseveres in the face of it all, even to the point of saying, "Though He will slay me, I will trust in Him" (Job 13:14).

From that moment on, the Cosmic Interveners have had their day. For suppose there were a Cosmic Intervener, one like Yahweh, who is disposed to test you because you are thoroughly decent. Would you remain decent even after he has destroyed all of your worldly loves and all of your accumulated defenses? And if so, what need do you have, in your robust decency, of such a debased being?

Yahweh, along with all the putative Cosmic Interveners, is rendered irrelevant by a faithfulness like Job's. Indeed, Job's trust looks as if it is already somehow directed toward a Higher One. Like Jeremiah, Job is already morally better than his god. It is Job, and not the Yahweh of Psalm 82, who brings about the true Götterdämmerung. (This is why we can at least understand the provocative exaggeration that Jung makes in his *Answer to Job*, namely, that Job's human and vulnerable faithfulness shows Yahweh that his best chance at spiritual development is to become a human being.)

Chapter 11

Christianity without Spiritual Materialism

Religion and Violence

Something remains that cries out for explanation, namely, the apparently nonaccidental connection between supernaturalist theism and religious violence: violence perpetrated in the name of God, and in the name of religions that avow justice and compassion. In raising this issue, we must not forget what the last century taught us all too many times, namely, that the deracinating effect of enforced state atheism can help unleash an unprecedented tide of blood; the crimes of Hitler, Stalin, Mao, and Pol Pot cannot be laid at the feet of monotheism. Better to have had "the haven of a heartless world" than the death camps, the pogroms, the endlessly destructive five-year plans, and the killing fields.

With that said, it must be added that any cold, hard look at supernaturalist theism presents us with a charnel house of religiously sanctioned, or, to be more accurate, religiously *required*, violence. Sacrifice, atonement, apocalypse, crusade, jihad (in the baser sense), all this followed by the exquisite tortures of hell; these are not accidents of supernaturalist theism perpetrated or imagined out of a *simple* misconstrual of its requirements.

To make the matter more specific, how is it, for example, that Christianity, allegedly born from the gospel of love, has fallen into the violence of crusades and inquisitions, and the vengeful threats of apocalypse and hell?

To get a feel for the thing to be explained, we are sometimes helped by beginning with an explanation; for even if the explanation is ultimately to be rejected, we may thereby get a better sense of the issue at hand. The most imaginative theologian of religious violence has been René Girard, and although his anthropological speculations must be wrong in some of their details, philosophers as different in outlook as

Roger Scruton and Gianni Vattimo have found in Girard such things as a profound replacement for the morally incoherent doctrine that by some kind of penal substitution Christ's torture and death propitiates the Highest One for the insult he felt at the sin of humanity.[1]

The Gospel according to Girard

Let us begin with Girard's best-titled book, *Des choses cachées depuis la fondation du monde,* in translation, *Things Hidden since the Foundation of the World.*[2] The title is taken from Matthew 13:35, "I will open my mouth in parables; I will utter things hidden since the foundation of the world." According to Girard, one main thing hidden since the foundation of the world is that social order, and particularly religiously legitimated social order, is based on murder, a particular sort of murder, the murder of the scapegoat, a murder whose function is to resolve, at least temporarily, the natural war of all against all.

That remarkable anthropological claim can be understood only in terms of Girard's equally remarkable psychology of desire. For Girard, humanity is a species of thoroughly *mimetic* animals. Born with a surplus of indeterminate yearning, human beings have to discover what to desire, at least when desire goes beyond the objects of their purely biological drives. They discover what to desire by imitating what others desire, so the things that seem most autonomous about us, most expressive of our individuality, namely, our heart's desires, have been borrowed from the others. Moreover, the indeterminate yearning of human beings is an expression not of inner fullness but of anxious emptiness; we experience ourselves as diminished by the other's possession of what we imitatively desire. This is the pattern of the playground, where a child with many toys wants the one toy that the other child has, and

1. See G. Vattimo, *After Christianity* (Columbia University Press, 2002), and R. Scruton, *Death-Devoted Heart: Sex and the Sacred in Wagner's Tristan and Isolde* (Oxford University Press, 2004).

2. *Things Hidden since the Foundation of the World*, with Jean-Michel Oughourlian and Guy Lefort, trans. Stephen Bann and Michael Metteer (Stanford University Press, 1987), a translation of *Des choses cachées depuis la fondation du monde* (1978). See also René Girard, *Violence and the Sacred*, trans. Patrick Gregory (Johns Hopkins University Press, 1977).

will not be happy without it; the same logic is manifest in the technique of making oneself more desirable by creating jealousy, and in many other forms of human rivalry.

The mimetic intensification of our battle for the objects of desire means that even in circumstances of economic surplus, we will still be rivals for the commonly desired objects. Inherent in unredeemed mimetic desire is the potential for a collective "mimetic" crisis, a Hobbesian war of all against all for the sake of possession of the common objects of desire. Girard proposes that primitive human communities must have experienced this awful internecine tension, and that the events that helped resolve the tension, however temporarily, were felt as a great cathartic deliverance. Girard theorizes that such cathartic deliverances constituted primitive religious experiences of group solidarity. He further supposes, on the basis of the anthropological record, and an imaginative reading of the history of extant mythology, that specifically the punishment of an accused scapegoat came to be a decisive way of resolving "mimetic" crises.

As with desire, hatred is also mimetic: we notice what the others hate, and hate it ourselves. In this way the stigmatized one can quickly become the object of a focused collective hatred. Thus the accused becomes the scapegoat. If that collective hatred leads to the expelling or murder of the scapegoat, there will then be an enormous cathartic release from the tension of the incipient war of all against all. The group has triumphed over the scapegoat and is unified in that triumph. But these acts need to be repeated, because the tension produced by ordinary mimetic desire inevitably returns.

In Girard's view, the practice of sacrificial ritual, in which an object or animal takes on the symbolic role of the scapegoat, emerges in anthropological history to deal with the recurrence of mimetic crises and the difficulty of continually finding actual scapegoats. It is ritualized sacrifice that now resolves the mutual hostile tension, and so the quasi-religious feeling of group solidarity, suddenly restored, attaches itself to the ritualized sacrifice.

Here we have the anthropological origins of religion, according to Girard. Sacrificial ritual has its origins in the incipient war of all against all, and in the hatred of the scapegoat. For such ritualized sacrificial religion to function as an antidote against individual rivalry, the violent origins of religion, and in particular religion's recurrent sanctioning of the violent sacrifice of the scapegoat, must be repressed.

And the rituals must be endlessly repeated, to serve the purpose of constantly lowering the tension produced by mimetic desire. The rituals do not transform the basic situation of humanity; they only help to make it tolerable.

Against this background the religion of Yahweh is a profound innovation, one that changes the very nature of human experience of the Divine. For it provides an entirely different way of resolving the mimetic crisis. Yahweh presents himself as an all-powerful Lawgiver, who offers a covenant to Israel, a special and intimate relation to him, if only they keep his commandments.

The force of the Mosaic Law is founded on Yahweh's immense power and might; his mercurial, even genocidal, tendencies toward those who flout his commands are crucial demonstrations of his determination to enforce his Law. They provide the coercive force behind an essentially juridical resolution to the mimetically generated acquisitive crisis. The juridical solution, resisting mimetic and hence covetous desire by Law, works best when the power of enforcement is concentrated in the hands of a single agent. (Compare Hobbes's account of the sovereign.) So monotheism arises, and survives, as a new form of religious solution to the mimetic crisis.

Now we can make sense of Girard's central claim: the real purpose of Christ's sacrifice and death is not to propitiate an angry or insulted Father-god, but to complete the movement begun in Yahweh's rejection of sacrifice, and finally bring sacrificial religion to an end. Christ comes, not to found a religion, but to unmask religion's origins in our most violent impulses, to render it no longer tenable as a solution to mimetically generated acquisitive tension, and finally to present a new, definitive resolution of the recurrent crisis.

Unredeemed mimetic desire is desire in which we encounter the well-being of others as a threat to our own well-being. (As Gore Vidal put the point: It is not enough to succeed; others must fail.) For Girard, this consequence of mimetic desire, and the role of religious violence in its resolution, is the expression of original sin, a pervasive orientation of sinfulness that exists prior to any particular sinful acts. The repetitive ritual discharge of acquisitive tension actually perpetuates this condition of sinfulness.

How, then, in Girard's view, does Christ overcome original sin?

First, Christ offers *himself* as a scapegoat; more exactly he provokes the Pharisees, collaborates with Judas in his own betrayal, and is coldly silent in front of Caiaphas but for his announcement that he will come in glory at the right hand of God. Second, Christ's Passion, itself a narrative re-creation of the victimizing of the scapegoat, is not to be understood as a sadomasochistic apotheosis offered to propitiate the just wrath of an otherwise unforgiving Father. It is the manifest demonstration that this scapegoat is innocent, as the words of the Roman centurion at the foot of the Cross reveal (see Luke 23:47). This already undermines the apparent legitimacy of sacrificial violence; but the death blow is delivered by the fact that in this case the innocent scapegoat is (according to Christian theology) the truly sacred One, namely, God himself.

To thus assimilate the significance of Christ's suffering and death would mean that we can never look at victims, even the victims of so-called legitimate violence, including the juridical violence of the state, in the same way. After the Cross, the face of God incarnate looks back at us from the image of the victim. Victimization, sacrifice, and religious violence have been forever unmasked as illegitimate strategies by which our murderous envy of each other is temporarily discharged, and yet preserved as an ongoing psychological orientation.

Notice that on Gerard's own view, this unmasking of so-called legitimate violence cannot in itself be a good thing, since without the ritualized sacrifice of the scapegoat, our original hostile impulses remain undischarged. To simply unmask the mechanism, and block the cathartic discharge, is to risk a full-scale mimetic crisis, a return to the war of all against all. But Christ offers something more, a new kind of mimesis: "give no thought to the morrow," that is, abandon the empty life of acquisitive desire, and "love one another as I have loved you"—and so take on the radical risk of being devoured by the others, as Christ was.

This is the salvation that Christ offers: the naked disclosure of our natural collective hatred and lust for violence, then freedom from the idea of *legitimate* violence, and, finally, a new resolution of the internecine mimetic tension, not by way of another temporary sacrificial discharge, but through the availability of a wholly new form of mimesis, the imitation of Christ's own self-sacrificing love.

So goes the brilliant Girardian story. As Girard's own title hints by omission, it is a parable, a kind of anthropological myth tailored to appropriately frame Christianity. If it has any appeal and power, as many find that it does, this must consist in the fact that Girard's story succeeds in framing Christianity as a very serious religious innovation, one that could indeed reach into the depth psychology of Jew and gentile alike, and capture them in a new transformative vision of how to live. That is not an easy thing to bring out. And without making that stand forth, we can make little sense of the extraordinary fervor of the early Jewish and gentile Christians, something testified to even by their enemies. That is, we can make little of the emergence of the phenomenon of Christianity.

But how can we know whether the clearly false elements in the Girardian frame are distorting or occluding central features of Christianity? Only by trying to do better, I suppose.

WHERE IS ORIGINAL SINFULNESS?

The criticisms of Girard's account of religion and of Christianity are by now commonplaces. The evidence for an anthropology of religion based exclusively on original murder is tenuous at best. Not all forms of nonbiological desire arise through imitation or mimesis. Nor is all religion sacrificial in nature. Nor is all religious sacrifice a form of scapegoating. Indeed, certain sacrificial rituals, such as the potlatch, are expressions of contempt for the commodity, the very thing that owes its aura of value to the triangulation of mimetic desire.

These criticisms, though correct, are relatively superficial, especially if I am right to hear in Girard's fabulous title his intention to talk in parables. A deeper criticism, a criticism capable of disabling Girard's framing parable *as a parable*, would be that he has misconstrued original sin and hence the salvific role of Christ. Before we turn to that, let us be clear on a central proposition that Girard's parable highlights: perhaps atonement by substitution, the placation of an insulted and angry Father God, is not what Christianity is really about.

Consider this question: Would there have been anything resembling Christianity, if at the end of his mission of healing and preaching, Christ had been bitten by a viper in the Garden of Gethsemane, and had suffered a slow and horribly painful death alone there in the Garden on the evening before what was to be Good Friday? No Passion and no Crucifixion; just death by viper, with the rest of the Gospel left in place. The debt of reparation for our sins might still have been paid by the death of the Son of God—imagine the agonizing death throes from the snakebite lasting hours—but the depth-psychological and salvific essence of Christianity *would never have come into the world*. Could anyone have turned to a religion of propitiation by viper bite as a serious source of salvation?

You will say there is more to it than that; there is, after all, the Resurrection.

But the Resurrection is not to the point here. For suppose that three days after a horrible death by viper bite, Christ rose from the dead. How would that help us? Are we not still lost? Are we not still dealing with a sort of farce, at least in comparison to what Christianity really is?

What, then, do the Passion and Crucifixion of Christ achieve that the viper (and the like) could not achieve? Answering that question may itself simply sideline the bizarre doctrine of substitutionary atonement, the paying off of our debt to God by the incarnation and horrible death of his Son.

Girard is one of the few theologians in whose work we can find any answer to this kind of question. Girard's answer is that the suffering and death of Christ are required to dramatically unmask and forever discredit the hidden structure of violence against the scapegoat, thereby rendering untenable sacrificial religion, the tension-discharging mechanism that helps preserve our original sinfulness. Death by viper bite might pay off our debt to an angry Father God, but it could not unmask and discredit sacrificial religion.

But what does our original sinfulness consist in, according to Girard? By nature we human beings rely upon a certain mechanism of learning what to desire; we learn this, in part, by imitation. This has an unfortunate consequence, namely, that even in conditions of economic surplus each desires what the other has, so there is always a certain level of competitive hostility in the air. By good or bad luck, a certain self-reinforcing mechanism of sacrificing the scapegoat comes to discharge this competitive tension. Religion is the symbolic repetition of this discharge mechanism. Religion's fault is twofold: it preserves the condition of competitive hostility, and it legitimates violence against the scapegoat.

Where is original sinfulness in this Girardian account? Does it lie in our needing to rely upon a certain method of learning? Surely not, for then the apes, too, would be in a condition of original sin, and who has come to save them? Is original sinfulness simply the envy that this method of learning produces? Not obviously: envy is one kind of sin (one of the seven deadly sins), but it emerges from our original sinfulness and is not the whole of it. Does original sinfulness then consist in the meliorating and violence-justifying character of religion? If that is so, then salvation consists merely in irreligion, as the undergraduate atheists have been urging all along.

Upon examination, it appears that there is no real *original sinfulness* in Girard, just an unfortunate response (sacrificial religion) to an unfortunate upshot (envy) of a method of learning (mimesis). If this were all we had to worry about, then Christ could come only as another exemplar of a better way, not as a savior who changes the whole frame of humanity by revealing the most frightening truth about us. Without original sinfulness, Christianity has no answer to the Greek idea that the ethical consists simply in the virtuous life, a life of excellence of character, which will itself drive out the excesses of envy and of violence. Christianity would be just an irrelevant complication, a jumbling up of human things.

Must we then understand original sinfulness as an insult to God, who then rightly claims a debt that only the torture of his Son can pay? No, that idea remains an atrocity committed upon the Highest One.

And it cannot explain why the viper bite could not have saved us.

ORIGINAL SINFULNESS AS SELF-WILL
AND FALSE RIGHTEOUSNESS

> But the serpent said to the woman, "You will surely not die. For
> God knows that when you eat of it your eyes will be opened, and
> you will be like God, knowing good and evil." So when the woman
> saw that the tree was good for food, and that it was a delight to
> the eyes, and that the tree was to be desired to make one wise, she
> took of its fruit and ate, and she also gave some to her husband
> who was with her, and he ate. (Genesis 3:3–7)

What was Eve's error, encouraged in her by the voice of cunning?
Eve's error had two facets: first, self-will, manifested in her disobedience
to Yahweh's command. But any disobedience would have manifested
that, and perhaps not any disobedience could have precipitated the Fall.
(Not even Yahweh is *that* touchy.) The form of Eve's disobedience also
seems crucial; and it seems overblown to call it envy of God. It was
driven by her anxious hope that "wisdom," a correct conception of
good and evil, and hence the knowledge of how to live, could be got
from a tree, off the shelf as it were—as if it were something fixed and
complete like an ideal commodity, as if it were something that could
be *possessed* by human beings. Our original sin thus consists in self-will
combined with the aspiration to possess the knowledge of how to live,
a false grasping after ready-to-wear righteousness, something that is
inherently compromised.

It is a myth, as everyone sensible says. As a myth, the sin of Eve and
Adam is to be interpreted not as an original event in history but as an
account of the original human predicament: an account of the cost of
being human. If the myth is any good, then to be human is to exhibit
the fallen condition dramatized in the myth. This is the sense in which
Eve is the mother of us all; she is the archetype of the human condition.

What the myth dramatizes as self-will and a false aspiration to finally
know how to live corresponds to our earlier naturalistic account of the
deeply problematic condition of the human being as the product of
augmenting the self-privileging that lies at the heart of the arena with
extended self-consciousness, awareness of the future, and the capacity

for symbolic thought. That combination produces self-will as a constant deliberative motif, along with a need for a guiding conception of the good to silence the emergent voice that demands that we *live our life*. Unfortunately, the guiding conception of the good can initially come only from a tree, from off the shelf, from what the others expect of us. And this means that our actual life is parceled out between two bad masters: our own self-will and a compromised conception of the good. How is it compromised? It is averaged out because commonly available, it is held to with a sense of false necessity, and it needs to be defended beyond its merits because otherwise we sense that we would have no idea of how we are to live. Indeed it must be defended, even with violence, for otherwise we would have to face the terror of discovering that we have no satisfactory way of being distinctively human, no good response to the voice that commands us to live our lives.

In fact our own self-will, our various defections from the other-regarding demands presented by our internalized conception of the good, already testifies to the intrinsic weakness of the conception; we know that it cannot fully command our own assent, so we know it must be policed in order that we may fend off the terror below.

What Girard makes so central, the mechanism of sacrificial scapegoating, is just one method of collectively policing violations of our common, compromised conception of how to live. But supernatural monotheism provides a more centralized resolution of this problem. Our compromised common conception of how to live is now delivered to us, and so underwritten by, none other than the Lord of the Universe. Is it any surprise, then, that the Lord of the Universe will, and indeed must, legitimate and cooperate in our violence against the infidels, the outsiders whose differently led lives threaten to testify to the radical contingency of our compromised conception of the good? And can he not also be expected to turn on us when we depart from (our common and compromised conception of) the good? And is it not natural to suppose that he can search every heart, to detect even the mere tendency to violation of the Law?

Now the strange character of Yahweh, the loving, jealous, and genocidal god, is no longer a mystery. He appears as the Lawgiver to "a stiff-necked people." He commands and sanctifies another compromised conception of how to live. For this to work, for it to prevent self-will from exposing the unsatisfactory nature of what is commanded, the Lawgiver has to make it known that he is not to be messed with, that he himself has an enormous capacity for retributive violence. Yahweh exactly fits the bill; this is why it would be utterly naive to bowdlerize the Hebrew scriptures, to omit or neglect Yahweh's immense cruelty, and emphasize only his justice, mercy, and love. That is to fail to understand the religious function of Yahweh. Yahweh *needs* to be an unpredictable threat if he is to successfully resolve the real crisis produced by original sinfulness, and so be a *god for men.*

Because policing the Law by searching the hearts of men is Yahweh's manner of being a god, he is able to repudiate the sacrificial rituals of the Israelites. Recall his dismissal of sacrifice:

> I hate, I despise your festivals, and I take no delight in your solemn assemblies. (Amos 5:21)

and again:

> I have had enough of burnt offerings of rams and the fat of fed beasts; I do not delight in the blood of bulls, or of lambs, or of goats. (Isaiah 1:11)

And then, against all odds, and here is the greatness of Judaism, Yahweh has a surprising second life; he evolves from the threatening giver and enforcer of the Law to the one whose prophets call for justice and mercy.

> When you stretch out your hands, I will hide my eyes from you. Even though you make many prayers, I will not listen; your hands are full of blood. Wash yourselves; make yourselves clean; remove the evil of your doings from before my eyes. Cease to do evil, learn to do good; seek justice, rescue the oppressed, defend the orphan, plead for the widow. (Isaiah 1:15–17)

Now the god repudiates the common conception of the good, the very one that he previously delivered and sanctified. In its place, what is commanded is a radical turn toward the real needs of others: seek justice, rescue the oppressed, defend the orphan, and plead for the widow. After this transformation in the god and what he commands, how could Christ add anything?

CHRIST DESTROYS THE KINGDOM OF SELF-WILL AND FALSE RIGHTEOUSNESS

There is an obvious thing about the Gospels that is seldom said, and when it is said, it is treated as a blasphemy. Christ is asking for it, almost from the very beginning of his mission. He continually provokes the legitimate religious authorities. He compares them to whitewashed sepulchers with rotting flesh within. He claims to be the living manifestation of the Highest One, thereby threatening Israel's covenantal privilege. He calls for the obliteration of family loyalty. His manner of speaking ("you have heard it said . . . but I say . . .") expresses a direct authority over the interpretation of scriptures and asserts the right to replace them with an allegedly more comprehensive understanding. He violently disrupts the commerce of the Temple, even though it is practically necessary as part of the provision of sacrificial animals. Even when Pilate tries to offer him something of a way out, he remains unhelpfully enigmatic, almost sullen.

His behavior is shocking, outrageous.

In a certain way, that is the point. Christ's behavior calls for a collective defense of the common and compromised conception of the good, and it receives it. The legitimate religious authorities, the guardians of righteousness, the defenders of the common conception that offers "the right way to live," are left with little choice. They mobilize the apparatus of the state and deliver an angry mob. Then the torture unto death begins. This is the narrative not of the scapegoat, but of the antinomian getting what he asked for, albeit in a brutal, all too brutal, world.

And yet Christianity says: This man was the Son of God, the most perfect manifestation of the Highest One. Absurd!

Absurd, but not because of the philosophical difficulties with the Incarnation and the like. (For these might well go away, given panentheism and a skillful deployment of the doctrine of analogy.) Absurd because if he was the Son of God, how could we ever again decently place our faith in any commonly legitimatized conception of how to live? Wouldn't the memory of that atrocity poison the very idea of full legitimacy, poison the very idea of ready-to-wear righteousness, of *possession* of the right way to live? We would have to accept that ready-to-wear righteousness has been exposed as by its nature always poised to defend itself against its own deepest anxiety, and pretty much at all cost, even to the point of destroying God.

After all, what does this absurdity that is Christ offer in place of righteous legitimacy? Not a way to live, certainly not in the sense of something that would allow a new form of ready-to-wear righteousness to be passed on, so as to make for a stable settlement with things. All that is offered instead are impossible commandments from out of the blue:

> Thou shalt love the Lord thy God with all thy heart, and with all thy soul, and with all thy mind, and with all thy strength: this is the first commandment. And the second is like it, namely this, Thou shalt love thy neighbor as thyself.

There it is. That is the choice. Make the safe bet, the one for which you cannot be blamed, because all the others are doing it: take upon yourself some form of ready-to-wear righteousness and gradually have it adjusted to your own proportions. Or radically abandon yourself to the will of God.

Worldly wisdom says: better to hand one's life over to a respectable conception of the good.

And yet, in the light of our understanding of the Fall, all such conceptions of the good would appear to be some version of the same bad fruit, that is, ready-to-wear righteousness; and so, given the dynamics that led to Christ's torture and death, they are under suspicion of always harboring the potential to produce "Strange Fruit" (in the shattering sense made famous by Billie Holiday).[3]

---

3. One performance is to be found at www.youtube.com/watch?v=h4ZyuULy9zs. Holiday appears to find the applause at the end an embarrassment, an attempt on the part of the audience to pretend that what they have just witnessed is a mere piece of entertainment. The words of the song are by Abel Meeropol, who along with his wife adopted the children of Julius and Ethel Rosenberg.

Let's back away from the jeremiad for a moment and return to our question: Why did Christ have to suffer and die at the hands of the legitimate religious and political authorities? Why wouldn't the viper have sufficed? Not, pace Gerard, because only then could the suffering and death of Christ be a reductio ad absurdum of scapegoating sacrifice, but because only then could it expose the mechanisms at the heart of false righteousness, this secret love of self-love trying at all costs to put down the anxiety about how to live, even to the point of murder. The Crucifixion discloses *how far we are prepared to go* in order to defend our idolatrous attachment to one or another adventitious form of righteousness.

This is the frightening truth revealed by Christ's suffering and death. This is why it is crucial for the existence of the depth-psychological and salvific world of Christianity that Christ be killed by "legitimate" state and religious violence.

In accord with this interpretation, Luke's narrative describes Christ's crucifixion as a bust; thanks to Christ's manifestly innocent demeanor on the Cross, the effect was not an exhilarating discharge. It was not even a sober collective conviction that justice had after all been done. It was an intense sense of collective shame:

> And when all the crowds who had gathered there for this spectacle saw what had taken place, they returned home, beating their breasts. (Luke 23:48)

This is the sense in which Christ destroys the *Kingdom* of self-love and false righteousness. Of course, it is not that the psychological power of self-love and false righteousness is actually diminished by the Passion and Crucifixion. Instead, self-love and false righteousness—that is to say, the central elements of the characteristically human form of life— no longer make up *a defensible realm*.

Contrast the death of Socrates. He also asks for it. He is a victim of those who would police the Athenian conception of respectability, an averaged-out conception of pious virtue. But Plato romanticizes the death of Socrates; his death is a fearless and noble suicide. Socrates talks philosophy until the very end; he is full of arguments for the soul, and even when he is not relying on these (bad) arguments, he remains convinced that the release from the body is a very desirable thing, some-thing that philosophy prepares us for. Socrates accepts the hemlock as a healing balm for the sickness that is life.

But suppose that instead he had to anticipate being stripped, beaten, and hung from a tree; how would the pose of nobility and fearlessness have held up then? Is there not something decadently twee about the death of Socrates as Plato presents it? And is this not connected with the calming doctrine of the afterlife, and with the corresponding idea of this life as a sickness that death heals?

Crucially, Plato's Socrates recognizes the legitimacy of the Athenian state; he accepts its claims upon him and so does not flee even in the face of an unjust sentence. In this way the death of Socrates secretly valorizes the false righteousness of Athenian respectability, by showing that even someone who really understands virtue will bow to this false righteousness in the end. Human ways of going on are secretly re-deemed by Plato's Socrates. The Kingdom of self-love and false righ-teousness remains legitimated.

The ordeal of Christ's Passion and Crucifixion is not at all like this. There is nothing noble or "humanly redeeming" about it, beginning as it does with his desperation in the Garden and ending with his despair on the Cross. It is not a cathartic tragedy. It leaves us at a total loss. We can return to human ways of going on only if we forget what happened. If we do not forget, we need to find a way to live that is not some form of self-love and false righteousness. And if we do not forget, we know that we cannot find this in ourselves. Then, and only then, are we prepared to take the two commandments, the salvation from with-out, seriously.

THE AFTERLIFE AS AN IDOLATROUS CONCEIT

Even if such a naturalistic construal of the Crucifixion is admitted, it will be said that panentheism, precisely because it is not supernaturalist, leaves no place for the afterlife, or for the Resurrection. The charge is only half-right.

Christ tells Pilate, "My Kingdom is not of this world." Ever since the first Christian writings we have in our possession, namely, the Epistles of Paul, the official line has been that Christ's Kingdom is therefore an otherworldly Kingdom, whose perfection we will find only in the afterlife.

However, that common supposition makes bad interpretive sense of the whole of John 18:36:

> Jesus answered, my Kingdom is not of this world: if my Kingdom were of this world, then would my servants fight, that I should not be delivered to the Jews: but my Kingdom is not from hence.

This cannot mean "My Kingdom is not of this world, but of the religious superworld." The angels of the superworld are well-equipped to fight, and they would prevail; why are they excluded as servants ready to fight? Indeed the contrastive distinction between "this world" and the religious superworld seems anachronistic when applied to John and the other Evangelists. Mark, as we saw, regarded the religious superworld as an animating part of "this world," and in that he was simply being a man of his time. So Christ's Kingdom, as it is spoken of here, is not a supernatural Kingdom, replete with special causal powers and agencies.

Suppose instead that Christ's Kingdom was merely an *unworldly* Kingdom, one in which the worldliness of self-love and false righteousness is shed in favor of *agape*: the love that Christ exhibits and commands, the love that looks for no return and so is extended even to one's enemies, the love that is the only authentic way to exit the world of acquisitive desire. Now this Kingdom is one that could come on earth, without the ministrations of any supernatural agency. Would Christ's message be in any way diminished—would he be less of an embodiment of the will of the Highest One—if it was only this Kingdom that he came to establish?

Paul answers yes, it would. For Paul and Pauline Christianity (if that is not a pleonasm), Christ's actual bodily resurrection prefigures what awaits us, namely, our own bodily resurrection and, if we have lived a Christ-centered life, eternal reward in the Kingdom of Heaven. If he ceased to believe in this, as he makes clear in his remarks to the Corinthians, *Paul himself would abandon Christ:*

But if it is preached that Christ has been raised from the dead, how can some of you say that there is no resurrection of the dead? If there is no resurrection of the dead, then not even Christ has been raised. And if Christ has not been raised, our preaching is useless and so is your faith. More than that, we are then found to be false witnesses about God, for we have testified about God that he raised Christ from the dead. But he did not raise him if in fact the dead are not raised. For if the dead are not raised, then Christ has not been raised either. And if Christ has not been raised, your faith is futile; you are still in your sins. Then those also who have fallen asleep in Christ are lost. If only for this life we have hope in Christ, we are to be pitied more than all men. But Christ has indeed been raised from the dead, the first fruits of those who have fallen asleep. (1Corinthians 15:12–20)

Whereas it took the vivid fear of death on the night before the Crucifixion to induce Peter to renounce Christ, Paul is prepared to do it, and prepared to urge his followers to do it, over a contentious point of metaphysics, the "bodily" resurrection: according to Paul a resurrection in which we all receive imperishable spiritual bodies in lieu of our corrupted physical bodies. The "bodily" resurrection, as Paul understands it, is not just a contentious point of metaphysics; it is a leftover of Paul's Pharisaical past. And yet he holds to it as a condition of Christ's being the savior.

Here we have the real despoliation of Christ.

One of the great signs that Judaism, despite all the depredations of the early Yahweh, remains a higher religion, is its relative indifference, excepting the tradition of the Pharisees, to the very idea of the afterlife. The references to any form of afterlife in the Hebrew Bible are few, and somewhat inconsistent in what they suggest it involves.

True, in Genesis, Enoch goes up to heaven to be with God, but this is obviously VIP treatment, and not something *ordinary* mortals can anticipate. Later Samuel is able to be contacted in the world of shades by a medium, and he tells Saul that he and his sons will join him there. Then there is Ezekiel 37:11–14:

They say "Our bones are dried up, and our hope is lost; we are cut off completely." Therefore prophesy, and say to them "Thus says the Lord God: I am going to open your graves and bring you up from your graves, and put my spirit within you." It is the Lord who speaks.

and the remark in the Isaianic Apocalypse:

Your dead shall live, their corpses shall rise. (Isaiah 26:19)

But scholars wonder whether in these two passages resurrection is simply used as a metaphor for the regeneration of Israel.

A clearly literal reference to life after death is found in Daniel 12:1–3, and yet it is not clearly a reference to bodily resurrection:

Many of those who sleep in the dust of the earth shall awake, some to everlasting life, and some to shame and everlasting contempt. Those who are wise shall shine like the brightness of the sky, and those who lead many to righteousness, like the stars for ever and ever.

(Interestingly, this theme in Daniel looks like a compensatory response to the slaughter of the Jewish martyrs in the Maccabean War. And the idea of *stellar* immortality is very likely of Hellenistic origin.)

Worse still for the provenance of Paul's Pharisaical idea of resurrection is the fact that the idea of resurrection, as a form of life after death, seems to have derived from the distinctly un-Christian notion of reincarnation, at least if we take seriously the reports of the first-century Jewish historian Flavius Josephus, who describes the Pharisees as believing that the souls of the righteous are reborn into other bodies. And in his account of the Essenes as Jewish followers of Pythagoras, Josephus describes what looks like their belief in reincarnation. This may be connected with the intermittent idea that the prophets are sometimes reincarnated, an idea that seems implicit in the answer the disciples give to Christ's question "Who do people say that I am?"

Some say John the Baptist; others say Elijah; and still others, Jeremiah or one of the prophets. (Matthew 16:14)

Again, this is still an idea of reincarnation, not of resurrection.

The various ideas of afterlife play two roles. The first is to provide a spiritual arena in which we can imagine our acquisitive desire being comprehensively slaked, even after death. So the dreary heaviness of the ancient Egyptian funeral system, with its intensively competitive preparations for the afterlife, stinks of unredeemed, indeed mummified, acquisitive desire simply projected onto the next world. The powers of the idol-gods of the Egyptian cult derive from their detailed roles as potential intermediaries and intercessory allies in the journey to the next world. In this way the whole of Egyptian religion is given life by death.

As against this first, and purely idolatrous, deployment of the idea of the afterlife, the question has always been: Why would another life of this sort answer any real question posed by this life? "Well, it will be a better life, at least if you obey the gods in this life!" But this idea of the next life as better is just the idea that we will finally attain *endless satisfaction* of our acquisitive desires. (Hence the silly promises of seventy doe-eyed virgins, all you can eat and drink forever, and so on and so forth.) The very idea of endless satisfaction of our acquisitive desires is a kind of contradiction. For our acquisitiveness arises from our sensed lack of being; unless that fundamental orientation changes, acquisitive desire cannot come to an end. And if by some grace that orientation were somehow changed *now*, the idolatrous version of the other world would thereby be rendered irrelevant.

Against "Man's Quest for Meaning"

Since the sixties (or is it the forties?) there has been a heady mix of popular existentialism and Judeo-Christian theology that represents the Highest One as utterly invested in something called man's quest for meaning, the drive to live a meaningful or significant life. Then comes the undeniable observation that there are things that can happen in life which undermine your chance of living a meaningful or significant life. So, the argument goes, do we not need an afterlife so that the Highest One can compensate us for such evils, provide us with further opportunities for a meaningful life, and thereby eventually (say, by way of final universal salvation) redeem his own huge investment in our quest for meaning?

I can say the kind of thing I believe Karl Barth would have said about this, and in roughly the same tone of voice. Man-centeredness! Idolatry! Most pernicious resistance to the will of God! The substitution of a local, historical human ideal for the ends of God! Let us put away childish things. God does not reveal himself in order to make it all better, but to offer us a salvation in which we are utterly transformed. Where does Christ say, "Follow me and you will live a meaningful life?" (That is what bad recruiters for seminaries would say, but where does Christ say that?)

But perhaps I have read Barth wrongly, or perhaps the gentle reader finds no natural authority in his theology, so here is what *I* would say.

The demand that you live a meaningful life is an inflated form of acquisitive desire and an ultimate reservation about how far you would go in modeling yourself on the kenotic self-abandonment that is God. Look instead to the self-disclosure of the Highest One as outpouring Life, Intelligibility, and Love, and find your life-ordering demands there. The quest for meaning is a local historical demand, one that arises under certain special conditions, and so one that it is not the business of Divinity to meet. That can seem false, if the demand for meaning is conflated with something else, namely, the demand of conscience, the demand that one live one's life out of some conception of the good. What is really bad, what could render one's life shameful or even not worth living, occurs when that conception of the good is shallow or perverted or confused. If God takes hold of us, then we will be safe from this. If he does not, then one's conception of the good will remain unredeemed.

Suppose, it will be objected, that this is because of one's own blameless incapacity. Then is not God unjust or devoid of power? But this is where we enter into childish things, a naive semantics of divine predication combined with a picture of God as a Cosmic Intervener.

Perhaps the crucial point can be made more directly. The idea of an afterlife that would make it finally all better, or at least finally very meaningful, depends on a radical underestimation of what can actually happen to you in this life. Salvation is not making it all better; it is the grace of finding a way to live that keeps faith with the importance of goodness and love even in the face of everything that can happen to you.

THE AFTERLIFE AS RESISTANCE TO CHRIST

Setting aside its role in empowering outright idolatry, the other function of the afterlife is the one that explains its emergence in Judaism, after the destruction of the First Temple, the humiliations of the Babylonian exile, and the slaughter of the Jewish faithful during the Maccabean War. Only an afterlife, it seems, can satisfy a demand for justice in the face of the highly accidental connection between being ethical and being happy. And when horrible circumstances make this disjunction sharply felt, the afterlife makes its appearance.

Kant turned these thoughts into the "moral argument" for the afterlife. To be ethical, Kant argued, is not to be happy—as Aristotle taught—but rather to *deserve* happiness; and it is a manifest fact that this world is not organized to reward the ethical life with happiness. As Ecclesiastes puts it,

> The battle does not always go to the strong, nor the race to the swift, nor bread to the wise, nor wealth to men of understanding. (Ecclesiastes, 9:11)

For Kant, the fact (if it is a fact) that being ethical is being *worthy* of happiness, imposes a further moral requirement on our wills: namely, that we should will the realization of a state—Kant calls it "The Highest Good" —in which ethical goodness and happiness converge. We have no reason to think that they will converge in our lifetimes, or indeed in this world. Yet we are rationally required to believe in the possibility of realizing the objects of our will. So, given the facts about this life, we are rationally required to hope for another life in which ethical conduct is properly rewarded.

Kant's second thought in favor of the afterlife is that without this hope we are naturally subject to moral discouragement. This is, anyway, how many do in fact react. Faced with the professional torturer who dies calmly in his sleep at a ripe old age, surrounded by his adoring family, and with the nurse who cared her whole life for the dying, only to herself die young and alone from a horribly painful and degrading illness, people tend to fall into despair over the importance of ethical goodness. Unless, that is, they have hope or faith.

In the third *Critique*, Kant illustrates his concern over moral discouragement by the example of Spinoza, in Kant's view a paradigm of a just man, one who actively revered the moral law, and so needed no promises or threats in order to be motivated to follow its commands. Yet Spinoza had no belief in individual immortality (Kant supposes), and so no belief that our earthly lives would be judged in the afterlife by a just God. So, according to Kant, Spinoza was susceptible to having his unselfish resolve to bring about the good undermined by consideration of the lives of other virtuous people and the manifest fact that

> [n]o matter how worthy of happiness they may be, nature, which pays no attention to that, will subject them all to the evils of deprivation, disease and untimely death. (*Critique of Judgment*, 452–53)

Kant allows himself a third variant on his theme of justice and the afterlife, perhaps the variant that is most relevant in an age in which the world financial system is run on principles of naked manipulation and legalized theft. Kant's third thought is that absent final justice, obedience to the moral law may simply turn the just into fodder for the predatory unjust. In the *Lectures on Ethics*, Kant writes:

> We are obliged to be moral. Morality implies a natural promise: otherwise it could not impose any obligation upon us. We owe obedience only to those who can protect us. Morality alone cannot protect us.[4]

4. Immanuel Kant, *Lectures on Ethics*, trans. Louis Infield (Hackett, 1981), 82.

Here the afterlife is presented not as the reason nor as the motive to be virtuous, but as a condition of virtue's making sense.

But now consider these Kantian arguments in the light of Christ's suffering and death. Suppose, for a moment, that we follow the historically immediate misinterpretation of those events, the one provided by the Epistle to the Hebrews, namely, that Christ's suffering and death constituted an exemplary propitiatory sacrifice made on our behalf. Then Christ would deserve a mighty compensation for his astonishing generosity, would he not? And, indeed, in Philippians 2:5–11, Paul quotes what seems to be an early Christian hymn that actually describes Christ's reward:

> Have the same mind in you as that of Christ Jesus: Who, being in very nature God, did not consider equality with God something to be grasped, but made himself nothing, taking the very nature of a servant, being made in human likeness. And being found in appearance as a man, he humbled himself and became obedient to death—even death on a cross! Therefore God exalted him to the highest place and gave him the name that is above every name, that at the name of Jesus every knee should bow, in heaven and on earth and under the earth.

Yet this attempt to assign a reward to Christ for his astounding suffering on our behalf is on its face incoherent. If Christ is the Son of God, he was always the Son of God, and he could never be elevated to a position beyond that status. The bending of the knee at his name would be nothing to him. It is thus impossible for Christ *to be rewarded* for what he has done. The very idea of Christ's reward makes no theological sense.

And it makes no sense when considered against the background of our previous account of the special significance of Christ's death and suffering. In undermining the Law, or righteousness, as the key to salvation, Christ's death killed off the idea of just desert under the Law, not as an ordinary moral idea, but as a viable salvific idea. (This is the import of the parables of the prodigal son, and of the helpers who came late in the day.) The new dispensation of Christ is founded on outpouring love, love that looks for nothing in return; it is not a dispensation of justice in which virtue must, in this life or the next, receive its reward.

So Kant's moral argument for life after death as the only way to achieve the requirements of just desert, an argument that goes back at least to the Wisdom of Solomon, has no force in the face of the suffering and death of Christ. Even if it were metaphysically possible to reward Christ for his astonishing suffering, this would represent a blind insult to the true achievement of Christ. But if rewarding Christ would be a profound misunderstanding of Christ's message, so also is looking to bodily resurrection (even in a spiritual body) *as our reward* for following Christ. Only if we clearly see that there can be no reward, does Christ's suffering and death bring our self-love and false righteousness to an end.

Spinoza, peace be upon *him*, wrote the following in one of his letters to his friend Henry Oldenburg, secretary of the Royal Society and founder of the *Philosophical Transactions*, the first true science journal:

> I therefore conclude, that the resurrection of Christ from the dead was in reality spiritual, and that to the faithful alone, according to their understanding, it was revealed that Christ was endowed with eternity, and had risen from the dead (using dead in the sense in which Christ said, "let the dead bury their dead"), giving by His life and death a matchless example of holiness. Moreover, He, to this extent, raises his disciples from the dead, in so far as they follow the example of His own life and death. It would not be difficult to explain the whole Gospel doctrine on this hypothesis. (Letter 23 in the Elwes selection of Spinoza's Correspondence)

Belief in the afterlife as a reward for faithfulness is either an idolatrous conceit or evidence of a failure to assimilate the radical nature of Christ's new dispensation.

Naturalism's Gift: Resurrection without the Afterlife

Spinoza may seem to be writing purely metaphorically of Christ's resurrection and that of his followers; but in fact he is not, for Spinoza actually derives from his own naturalism the remarkable result that there is some part of the human mind that is eternal.[5] (There is a certain affinity between Spinoza's view and the previous account of Objective Mind.) Spinoza's route to the eternity of the mind is too difficult to rehearse here, but it at least shows that naturalism itself does not obviously *entail* that death is the end.

Indeed, legitimate naturalism itself opens up an intriguing theological possibility. Most surprisingly, the way beyond death can be found in naturalism's denial of the soul, that is, in the empirical discovery that at the core of our mental lives there are no separately existing entities, distinct from our brains and bodies, whose persistence constitutes our personal identity over time.[6] The realization that there is no separately existing entity distinct from our brains and bodies can be seen to lead to the discovery that our personal identity over time is actually *secured* by certain patterns of personal identification with what then become our future selves.

Consider the structure of future directed self-concern. When you think of a person in the future as yourself, you conceive of him or her in a way that makes his or her anticipatable interests and needs default starting points in your present practical reasoning. You can then just begin from his or her anticipatable interests, and immediately find them to be grounds for your present preference and action. And you can do this nonderivatively, that is, without the mediation of moral principle, or fellow feeling toward yourself, or even self-admiration. You don't even need to particularly like your anticipated future self. It is just that his or her interests directly figure as reasons for you now. Call this special concern for a future person. It is the typical structure found in the special concern each one has for him- or herself. Special *self*-concern is just this pattern of special concern directed toward a person one takes to be oneself.

The demise of the soul, and hence of the self, means that the extent and focus of one's special concern is not antecedently justified by an independently persisting entity that itself determines the temporal

---

5. "Eternity" expresses a highly developed and technical notion in Spinoza, which in no way compromises Spinoza's thoroughgoing rejection of supernaturalism.

6. Compare pt. 3 of Derek Parfit's *Reasons and Persons* (Oxford University Press, 1984). My differences with Parfit are discussed in detail in lecture 5 of *Surviving Death*.

and spatial extent of who we are. Rather, our temporal and spatial extent is determined by our pattern of special concern. This is the new "Copernican Revolution" induced by naturalism's (re)discovery that there is no self behind our mental functioning. The independent facts of personal identity do not justify our patterns of self-concern; rather, the facts of personal identity are partly determined by those patterns of self-concern.

Given that, the central commandment of Christianity—to love one's neighbor, indeed even one's enemies, as oneself—is nothing less than an *identity-reconstituting* command. The command is Janus-faced: it requires that one love the arbitrary other as oneself, but it also requires that one love oneself objectively; that is, as just the arbitrary other whose life one is nonetheless called upon to lead.

In my Hempel Lectures, *Surviving Death*, I have set about arguing in detail that to the extent that one carries out this commandment, one becomes present wherever and whenever human beings are present; one lives on in the onward rush of humankind and acquires a new face every time a baby is born. For one stands to all others in the identity-constituting relation that one formerly stood in just to oneself.[7]

Here we can only leave that as a mere intimation of how those who live the life of *agape* might live on in the onward rush of humanity. Perhaps in this way, even naturalists can make literal sense of John Stuart Mill's conclusion to his great essay "The Utility of Religion." There Mill writes:

> I am now speaking of the unselfish. Those who are so wrapped up in self that they are unable to identify their feelings with anything which will survive them, or to feel their life prolonged in their younger contemporaries and in all who help to carry on the progressive movement of human affairs, require the notion of another selfish life beyond the grave, to enable them to keep up any interest in existence, since the present life, as its termination approaches, dwindles into something too insignificant to be worth caring about. But if the Religion of Humanity were as sedu-

7. See lectures 4 and 5 of *Surviving Death*.

lously cultivated as the supernatural religions are (and there is no difficulty in conceiving that it might be much more so), all who had received the customary amount of moral cultivation would up to the hour of death live ideally in the life of those who are to follow them.[8]

In any case, we can now see how it could be that Christ is resurrected, as "the first fruit" of the collective victory over death of those who are truly good. Christ conquers death on our behalf by ideally exemplifying *agape*, and stimulating it in us.

8. Mill, *Three Essays on Religion*, 119.

Postscript

Better to end in the middle of things than create a false impression of completeness, or the aspiration to completeness.

Our exploration of the ban on idolatry has led us to an idea of the Most High as the one whose transcendence is just the other side of his immanence in this world. This world, properly seen, is the outpouring and self-disclosure that is the Highest One. This outpouring and self-disclosure, this *kenosis* or self-emptying of Being that envelops everything, is the site of the sacred. So we are "already on holy ground." A saved human being is just a finite manifestation of the *kenosis*, filled with an awareness of itself as such, an awareness made manifest in that human being's turn toward reality and the real needs of others.

For one who is saved, the glory *that is* negates the necessity of the glory to come. There need be no next world. There need be no heavenly antechamber where the decisive events of spiritual history occur. These ideas may just be leftovers from the superstitious and idolatrous attempts to placate spiritual powers and principalities.

There is, however, *another* world—it is this world properly received.

Index